THE SIMPLETON
THE SIX
THE MILLIONAIRESS

LONDON

PUBLISHED BY

Constable and Company Ltd.

10–12 ORANGE STREET W.C.2

•

INDIA

Orient Longmans Ltd.

BOMBAY   CALCUTTA   MADRAS

•

CANADA

Longmans, Green and Company

TORONTO

ʼ

SOUTH AND EAST AFRICA

Longmans, Green and Company Ltd.

CAPE TOWN   NAIROBI

THE SIMPLETON, THE SIX, AND THE MILLIONAIRESS. BEING THREE MORE PLAYS BY BERNARD SHAW

LONDON
CONSTABLE AND COMPANY
LIMITED

First published *1936*
Reprinted *1949*
Reprinted *1953*

PRINTED IN GREAT BRITAIN
BY R. & R. CLARK, LIMITED, EDINBURGH

CONTENTS

v

THE SIMPLETON OF
THE UNEXPECTED ISLES

XLV

1934

PREFACE ON DAYS OF JUDGMENT

THE increasing bewilderment of my journalist critics as to why I should write such plays as The Simpleton culminated in New York in February 1935, when I was described as a dignified old monkey throwing coco-nuts at the public in pure senile devilment. This is an amusing and graphic description of the effect I produce on the newspapers; but as a scientific criticism it is open to the matter-of-fact objection that a play is not a coco-nut nor I a monkey. Yet there is an analogy. A coco-nut is impossible without a suitable climate; and a play is impossible without a suitable civilization. If author and journalist are both placid Panglossians, convinced that their civilization is the best of all possible civilizations, and their countrymen the greatest race on earth: in short, if they have had a university education, there is no trouble: the press notices are laudatory if the play is entertaining. Even if the two are pessimists who agree with Jeremiah that the heart of man is deceitful above all things and desperately wicked, and with Shakespear that political authority only transforms its wielders into angry apes, there is still no misunderstanding; for that dismal view, or a familiar acquaintance with it, is quite common.

Such perfect understanding covers much more than nine hundred and ninety cases out of every thousand new plays. But it does not cover the cases in which the author and the journalist are not writing against the same background. The simplest are those in which the journalist is ignorant and uncultivated, and the author is assuming a high degree of knowledge and culture in his audience. This occurs oftener than it should; for some newspaper editors think that any reporter who has become stage struck by seeing half a dozen crude melodramas is thereby qualified to deal with Sophocles and Euripides, Shakespear and Goethe, Ibsen and Strindberg, Tolstoy and Tchekov, to say nothing of myself. But the case with which I am concerned here is one in which a reasonably well equipped critic shoots wide

3

because he cannot see the target nor even conceive its existence. The two parties have not the same vision of the world. This sort of vision varies enormously from individual to individual. Between the superstatesman whose vision embraces the whole politically organized world, or the astronomer whose vision of the universe transcends the range of our utmost telescopes, and the peasant who fiercely resists a main drainage scheme for his village because others as well as he will benefit by it, there are many degrees. The Abyssinian Danakil kills a stranger at sight and is continually seeking for an excuse to kill a friend to acquire trophies enough to attract a wife. Livingstone risked his life in Africa every day to save a black man's soul. Livingstone did not say to the sun colored tribesman "There is between me and thee a gulf that nothing can fill": he proposed to fill it by instructing the tribesman on the assumption that the tribesman was as capable mentally as himself, but ignorant. That is my attitude when I write prefaces. My newspaper critics may seem incapable of anything better than the trash they write; but I believe they are capable enough and only lack instruction.

I wonder how many of them have given serious thought to the curious changes that take place in the operation of human credulity and incredulity. I have pointed out on a former occasion that there is just as much evidence for a law of the Conservation of Credulity as of the Conservation of Energy. When we refuse to believe in the miracles of religion for no better reason fundamentally than that we are no longer in the humor for them we refill our minds with the miracles of science, most of which the authors of the Bible would have refused to believe. The humans who have lost their simple childish faith in a flat earth and in Joshua's feat of stopping the sun until he had finished his battle with the Amalekites, find no difficulty in swallowing an expanding boomerang universe. They will refuse to have their children baptized or circumcized, and insist on their being vaccinated, in the teeth of overwhelming evidence that vaccination has killed thousands of children in a quite horrible way whereas no child has ever been a penny the worse for baptism

4

since John the Baptist recommended it. Religion is the mother of scepticism: Science is the mother of credulity. There is nothing that people will not believe nowadays if only it be presented to them as Science, and nothing they will not disbelieve if it be presented to them as religion. I myself began like that; and I am ending by receiving every scientific statement with dour suspicion whilst giving very respectful consideration to the inspirations and revelations of the prophets and poets. For the shift of credulity from religious divination to scientific invention is very often a relapse from comparatively harmless romance to mischievous and even murderous quackery.

Some credulities have their social uses. They have been invented and imposed on us to secure certain lines of behavior as either desirable for the general good or at least convenient to our rulers. I learned this early in life. My nurse induced me to abstain from certain troublesome activities by threatening that if I indulged in them the cock would come down the chimney. This event seemed to me so apocalyptic that I never dared to provoke it nor even to ask myself in what way I should be the worse for it. Without this device my nurse could not have ruled me when her back was turned. It was the first step towards making me rule myself.

Mahomet, one of the greatest of the prophets of God, found himself in the predicament of my nurse in respect of having to rule a body of Arab chieftains whose vision was not co-extensive with his own, and who therefore could not be trusted, when his back was turned, to behave as he himself would have behaved spontaneously. He did not tell them that if they did such and such things the cock would come down the chimney. They did not know what a chimney was. But he threatened them with the most disgusting penances in a future life if they did not live according to his word, and promised them very pleasant times if they did. And as they could not understand his inspiration otherwise than as a spoken communication by a personal messenger he allowed them to believe that the angel Gabriel acted as a celestial postman between him and Allah, the fountain of all inspiration. Except in this way he could not have made them believe in anything but sacred stones and the seven deadly sins.

The Christian churches and the Christian Kings were driven to the same device; and when I evolved beyond the cock and chimney stage I found myself possessed with a firm belief that all my Roman Catholic fellow children would inevitably burn in blazing brimstone to all eternity, and even that I myself, in spite of my Protestant advantages, might come to the same endless end if I were not careful. The whole civilized world seemed to be governed that way in those days. It is so to a considerable extent still. A friend of mine lately asked a leading Irish statesman why he did not resort to a rather soulless stroke of diplomacy. Because, replied the statesman, I happen to believe that there is such a place as hell.

Anywhere else than in Ireland the obsolescence of this explanation would have been startling. For somehow there has been a shift of credulity from hell to perishing suns and the like. I am not thinking of the humanitarian revolt against everlasting brimstone voiced by the late Mrs Bradlaugh Bonner, nor of Tolstoy's insistence on the damnation on earth of the undetected, unpunished, materially prosperous criminal. I am leaving out of the question also the thoughtful, sentimental, honorable, conscientious people who need no hell to intimidate them into considerate social behavior, and who have naturally outgrown the devil with his barbed tail and horns just as I outgrew the cock in the chimney.

But what of the people who are capable of no restraint except that of intimidation? Must they not be either restrained or, as the Russians gently put it, liquidated. No State can afford the expense of providing policemen enough to watch them all continually; consequently the restraint must, like the fear of hell, operate when nobody is looking. Well, a shift of credulity has destroyed the old belief in hell. How then is the social work previously done by that belief to be taken up and carried on? It is easy to shirk the problem by pointing out that the belief in hell did not prevent

6

even the most superstitious people from committing the most damnable crimes. But though we know of these failures of infernal terrorism we have no record of its successes. We know that naïve attempts to bribe divine justice led to a trade in absolutions, pardons, and indulgences which proved by the hardness of the cash the sinners put down and the cost of the cathedrals they put up that there was a continual overdrawing of salvation accounts by firm believers in the brimstone; but we do not know, and never shall know, how many crimes were refrained from that would have been committed but for the dread of damnation. All we can do is to observe and grapple with the effect of the shift of credulity which has robbed hell of its terrors.

No community, however devout, has ever trusted wholly to damnation and excommunication as deterrents. They have been supplemented by criminal codes of the most hideous barbarity (I have been contemporary with Europeans whose amusements included seeing criminals broken on the wheel). Therefore their effect on conduct must be looked for in that very extensive part of it which has not been touched by the criminal codes, or in which the codes actually encourage anti-social action and penalize its opposite, as when the citizen is forced by taxation or compulsory military service to become an accomplice in some act of vulgar pugnacity and greed disguised as patriotism.

Unless and until we get a new column in the census papers on the point we can only guess how far the shift of credulity has actually taken place in countries like our own in which children, far from being protected against the inculcation of the belief in brimstone, are exposed to it in every possible way, and are actually, when they have been confirmed, legally subject to ruinous penalties for questioning it. It happens, however, that in one of the largest States in the world, Russia, the children are protected from proselytizing (otherwise than by the State itself) not only by the negative method called Secular Education, but by positive instruction that there is no personal life after death for the individual, the teaching being that of Ecclesiastes in our own canon "Whatsoever thy hand findeth to do, do it with thy might;

for there is no work, nor device, nor knowledge, nor wisdom, in the grave whither thou goest." We may take it that no civilized Russian born within the last twenty years has any apprehension of having to suffer after death for sins committed before it. At the same time the list of activities blacklisted by the Russian State as felonious has been startlingly extended; for the Russian Government has turned the country's economic morals downside up by breaking away from our Capitalist Utopia and adopting instead the views of the Bolshevist prophets whose invectives and warnings fill the last books of the Old Testament, and the Communist principles of Jesus, Peter, and Paul. Not that the Soviet Republic allows the smallest authority to Jesus or Peter, Jeremiah or Micah the Morasthite. They call their economic system, not Bolshevik Christianity, but Scientific Socialism. But as their conclusions are the same, they have placed every Russian under a legal obligation to earn his own living, and made it a capital crime on his part to compel anyone else to do it for him. Now outside Russia the height of honor and success is to be a gentleman or lady, which means that your living is earned for you by other people (mostly untouchables), and that, far from being under an obligation to work, you are so disgraced by the mere suggestion of it that you dare not be seen carrying a parcel along a fashionable thoroughfare. Nobody has ever seen a lady or gentleman carrying a jug of milk down Bond Street or the *rue de la Paix*. A white person doing such a thing in Capetown would be socially ruined. The physical activities called Sport, which are needed to keep the gentry in health, must be unpaid and unproductive: if payment is accepted for such activities the payee loses caste and is no longer called Mister. Labor is held to be a cross and a disgrace; and the lowest rank known is that of laborer. The object of everyone's ambition is an unearned income; and hundreds of millions of the country's income are lavished annually on ladies and gentlemen whilst laborers are underfed, ill clothed, and sleeping two or three in a bed and ten in a room.

Eighteen years ago this anti-labor creed of ours was the established religion of the whole civilized world. Then suddenly, in one seventh of that world, it was declared a damnable heresy, and had to be rooted out like any other damnable heresy. But as the heretics were carefully taught at the same time that there is no such thing as damnation, how were they to be dealt with? The well-to-do British Liberal, clamoring for freedom of conscience, objects to heretics being restrained in any way: his panacea for that sort of difficulty is Toleration. He thinks that Quakers and Ritualists should tolerate oneanother; and this solution works quite well because it does not now matter a penny to the State or the individual whether a citizen belongs to one persuasion or the other. But it was not always so. George Fox, the heroic founder of the Quakers, could not hear a church bell without dashing into the church and upsetting the service by denouncing the whole business of ritual religion as idolatrous. The bell, he said, "struck on his heart." Consequently it was not possible for the Churches to tolerate George Fox, though both Cromwell and Charles II liked the man and admired him.

Now the heretic in Russia is like Fox. He is not content with a quiet abstract dissent from the State religion of Soviet Russia: he is an active, violent, venomous saboteur. He plans and carries out breakages of machinery, falsifies books and accounts to produce insolvencies, leaves the fields unsown or the harvests to rot unreaped, and slaughters farm stock in millions even at the cost of being half starved (sometimes wholly starved) by the resultant "famine" in his fanatical hatred of a system which makes it impossible for him to become a gentleman. Toleration is impossible: the heretic-saboteur will not tolerate the State religion; consequently the State could not tolerate him even if it wanted to.

This situation, though new to our generation of Liberal plutocrats, is not new historically. The change from paganism and Judaism to Christianity, from the worship of consecrated stones to an exalted monotheism under Mahomet, and from world catholicism to national individualism at the Reformation, all led to the persecution and virtual outlawry of the heretics who would not accept the change. The original official Roman Catholic Church, which had perhaps the toughest job, was com-

9

pelled to develop a new judicial organ, called the Inquisition or Holy Office, to deal with heresy; and though in all the countries in which the Reformation triumphed the Inquisition became so unpopular that its name was carefully avoided when similar organs were developed by the Protestant and later on by the Secularist governments, yet the Holy Office cropped up again under all sorts of disguises. Protestant England would never have tolerated the Star Chamber if it had called itself an Inquisition and given Laud the official title borne by Torquemada. In the end all the specific Inquisitions petered out, not in the least through a growth of real tolerance, but because, as the world settled down into the new faiths, and the heretics stopped sabotaging and slaughtering, it was found that the ordinary courts could do all the necessary persecution, such as transporting laborers for reading the works of Thomas Paine, or imprisoning poor men for making sceptical jokes about the parthenogenesis of Jesus.

Thus the Inquisition came to be remembered in England only as an obsolete abomination which classed respectable Protestants with Jews, and burned both. Conceive, then, our horror when the Inquisition suddenly rose up again in Russia. It began as the Tcheka; then it became the Gay-pay-oo (Ogpu); now it has settled down as part of the ordinary police force. The worst of its work is over: the heretics are either liquidated, converted, or intimidated. But it was indispensable in its prime. The Bolsheviks, infected as they were with English Liberal and Agnostic notions, at first tried to do without it; but the result was that the unfortunate Commissars who had to make the Russian industries and transport services work, found themselves obliged to carry pistols and execute saboteurs and lazy drunkards with their own hands. Such a Commissar was Djerjinsky, now, like Lenin, entombed in the Red Square. He was not a homicidally disposed person; but when it fell to his lot to make the Russian trains run at all costs, he had to force himself to shoot a station master who found it easier to drop telegrams into the waste paper basket than to attend to them. And it was this gentle Djerjinsky who, unable to endure the duties of an executioner (even had he had time for them), organized the Tcheka.

Now the Tcheka, being an Inquisition and not an ordinary police court dealing under written statutes and established precedents with defined offences, and sentencing the offenders to prescribed penalties, had to determine whether certain people were public spirited enough to live in a Communist society, and, if not, to blow their brains out as public nuisances. If you would not work and pull your weight in the Russian boat, then the Tcheka had to make you do it by convincing you that you would be shot if you persisted in your determination to be a gentleman. For the national emergencies were then desperate; and the compulsion to overcome them had to be fiercely in earnest.

I, an old Irishman, am too used to Coercion Acts, suspensions of the Habeas Corpus Act, and the like, to have any virtuous indignation left to spare for the blunders and excesses into which the original Tcheka, as a body of well intentioned amateurs, no doubt fell before it had learnt the limits of its business by experience. My object in citing it is to draw attention to the legal novelty and importance of its criterion of human worth. I am careful to say legal novelty because of course the criterion must have been used in the world long before St Paul commanded that "if any would not work, neither should he eat." But our courts have never taken that Communist view: they have always upheld unconditional property, private property, real property, do-what-you-like-with-your-own property, which, when it is insanely extended to the common earth of the country, means the power to make landless people earn the proprietors' livings for them. Such property places the social value of the proprietor beyond question. The propertyless man may be challenged as a rogue and a vagabond to justify himself by doing some honest work; but if he earns a gentleman's living for him he is at once vindicated and patted on the back. Under such conditions we have lost the power of conceiving ourselves as responsible to society for producing a full equivalent of what we consume, and indeed more. On the contrary, every inducement to shirk that primary duty is continually before us. We are taught to think of an Inquisition as a tribunal which has to decide whether we accept the divinity of Christ or are Jews, whether we believe in transubstantiation or merely in the Supper, whether we are prelatists or Presbyterians, whether we accept the authority of the Church or the conclusions of our private judgments as the interpreters of God's will, whether we believe in a triune godhead or a single one, whether we accept the 39 Articles or the Westminster Confession, and so on. Such were the tests of fitness to live accepted by the old Inquisitions. The public never dreams of an economic test except in the form of a Means Test to baffle the attempts of the very poor to become sinecurists like ladies and gentlemen.

My own acquaintance with such a possibility began early in life and shocked me somewhat. My maternal grandfather, a country gentleman who was an accomplished sportsman, was out shooting one day. His dog, growing old, made a mistake: its first. He instantly shot it. I learnt that he always shot his sporting dogs when they were past their work. Later on I heard of African tribes doing the same with their grandparents. When I took seriously to economic studies before electric traction had begun I found that tramway companies had found that the most profitable way of exploiting horses was to work them to death in four years. Planters in certain districts had found the like profitable term for slaves to be eight years. In fully civilized life there was no provision except a savagely penal Poor Law for workers thrown out of our industrial establishments as "too old at forty."

As I happen to be one of those troublesome people who are not convinced that whatever is is right these things set me thinking. My thoughts would now be attributed to Bolshevik propaganda; and pains would be taken by our rulers to stop the propaganda under the impression that this would stop the thoughts; but there was no Bolshevik propaganda in those days; and I can assure the Foreign Office that the landed gentry in the person of my grandfather, the tramway companies, and the capitalist planters, made the question of whether individual dogs and men are worth their salt familiar to me a whole generation before the Tcheka ever existed.

PREFACE

It still seems to me a very pertinent question, as I have to pay away about half my earnings in tribute to the lady-and-gentleman business in order to get permission to live on this earth; and I consider it money very ill spent. For if the people who live on my earnings were changed by some Arabian Nights magician into dogs, and handed over to the sporting successors of my grandfather, they would be shot; and if they were changed into horses or slaves they would be worn out by overwork before their natural time. They are now worn out by underwork.

Nevertheless I do not plead a personal grievance, because though I still amuse myself with professional pursuits and make money by them, I also have acquired the position of a gentleman, and live very comfortably on other people's earnings to an extent which more than compensates me for the depredations of which I am myself the victim. Now my grandfather's dog had no such satisfaction. Neither had the tramway horses nor the slaves, nor have the discarded "too old at forty." In their case there was no proper account keeping. In the nature of things a human creature must incur a considerable debt for its nurture and education (if it gets any) before it becomes productive. And as it can produce under modern conditions much more than it need consume it ought to be possible for it to pay off its debt and provide for its old age in addition to supporting itself during its active period. Of course if you assume that it is no use to itself and is there solely to support ladies and gentlemen, you need not bother about this: you can just leave it to starve when it ceases to be useful to its superiors. But if, discarding this view, you assume that a human creature is created for its own use and should have matters arranged so that it shall live as long as it can, then you will have to go into people's accounts and make them all pay their way. We need no Bolshevik propaganda to lead us to this obvious conclusion; but it makes the special inquisitionary work of the Tcheka intelligible. For the Tcheka was simply carrying out the executive work of a constitution which had abolished the lady and gentleman exactly as the Inquisition carried out the executive work of a catholic constitution which had abolished

13

Jupiter and Diana and Venus and Apollo.

Simple enough; and yet so hard to get into our genteel heads that in making a play about it I have had to detach it altogether from the great Russian change, or any of the actual political changes which threaten to raise it in the National-Socialist and Fascist countries, and to go back to the old vision of a day of reckoning by divine justice for all mankind.

Now the ordinary vision of this event is almost pure bugaboo: we see it as a colossal Old Bailey trial, with the good people helped up into heaven and the bad ones cast headlong into hell; but as to what code of law will govern the judgment and classify the judged as sheep or goats as the case may be, we have not troubled to ask. We are clear about Judas Iscariot going to hell and Florence Nightingale to heaven; but we are not so sure about Brutus and Cromwell. Our general knowledge of mankind, if we dare bring it into play, would tell us that an immense majority of the prisoners at the bar will be neither saints nor scoundrels, but borderland cases of extreme psychological complexity. It is easy to say that to divine justice nothing is impossible; but the more divine the justice the more difficult it is to conceive how it could deal with every case as one for heaven or hell. But we think we need not bother about it; for the whole affair is thought of as a grand finish to the human race and all its problems, leaving the survivors in a condition of changeless unprogressive bliss or torment for the rest of eternity.

To me this vision is childish; but I must take people's minds as I find them and build on them as best I can. It is no use my telling them that their vision of judgment is a silly superstition, and that there never will be anything of the kind. The only conclusion the pious will draw is that I, at all events, will go to hell. As to the indifferent and the sceptical, I may do them the mischief against which Jesus vainly warned our missionaries. I may root out of their minds the very desirable conception that they are all responsible to divine justice for the use they make of their lives, and put nothing in its place except a noxious conceit in their emancipation and an exultant impulse to abuse it. The substitution of irresponsibility for responsibility may present itself as an advance; but it is in fact a retreat which may leave its victim much less eligible as a member of a civilized community than the crudest Fundamentalist. A prudent banker would lend money on personal security to Bunyan rather than to Casanova. Certainly I should if I were a banker.

Who shall say, then, that an up-to-date Vision of Judgment is not an interesting subject for a play, especially as events in Russia and elsewhere are making it urgently desirable that believers in the Apocalypse should think out their belief a little? In a living society every day is a day of judgment; and its recognition as such is not the end of all things but the beginning of a real civilization. Hence the fable of The Simpleton of the Unexpected Isles. In it I still retain the ancient fancy that the race will be brought to judgment by a supernatural being, coming literally out of the blue; but his inquiry is not whether you believe in Tweedledum or Tweedledee but whether you are a social asset or a social nuisance. And the penalty is liquidation. He has appeared on the stage before in the person of Ibsen's button moulder. And as history always follows the stage, the button moulder came to life as Djerjinsky. My Angel comes a day after the fair; but time enough for our people, who know nothing of the button moulder and have been assured by our gentleman-ladylike newspapers that Djerjinsky was a Thug.

The button moulder is a fiction; and my Angel is a fiction. But the pressing need for bringing us to the bar for an investigation of our personal social values is not a fiction. And Djerjinsky is not a fiction. He found that as there are no button moulders and no angels and no heavenly tribunals available, we must set up earthly ones, not to ascertain whether Mr Everyman in the dock has committed this or that act or holds this or that belief, but whether he or she is a creator of social values or a parasitical consumer and destroyer of them.

Unfortunately the word tribunal immediately calls up visions not only of judgment but of punishment and cruelty. Now there need be no more question of either of these abominations than there was in the case of my grandfather's dog. My grandfather would have been horribly ashamed of himself if the dog's death had not been instantaneous and unanticipated. And the idea of punishment never entered either his mind or the dog's. (Djerjinsky, by the way, is believed to have devised a similar method of painless liquidation.) It may be expedient that one man should die for the people; but it does not follow in the least that he should be tortured or terrified. Public savagery may demand that the law shall torment a criminal who does something very provoking; for the Sermon on The Mount is still a dead letter in spite of all the compliments we pay it. But to blow a man's brains out because he cannot for the life of him see why he should not employ labor at a profit, or buy things solely to sell them again for more than he gave for them, or speculate in currency values: all of them activities which have for centuries enjoyed the highest respectability, is an innovation which should be carried out with the utmost possible delicacy if public opinion is to be quite reconciled to it. We have also to reckon with the instinctive shrinking from outright killing which makes so many people sign petitions for the reprieve of even the worst murderers, and take no further interest if a reprieve decrees that their lives shall be taken by the slow torture of imprisonment. Then we have a mass of people who think that murderers should be judicially killed, but that the lives of the most mischievous criminals should be held sacred provided they do not commit murder. To overcome these prejudices we need a greatly increased intolerance of socially injurious conduct and an uncompromising abandonment of punishment and its cruelties, together with a sufficient school inculcation of social responsibility to make every citizen conscious that if his life costs more than it is worth to the community the community may painlessly extinguish it.

The result of this, however, will finally be a demand for codification. The citizen will say "I really must know what I may do and what I may not do without having my head shot off." The reply "You must keep a credit balance always at the national bank" is sufficiently definite if the national accountancy is trustworthy and compulsory unemployment made impossible. In fact it is so definite that it finally takes the matter out of the hands of the Inquisition and makes an overdraft an ordinary offence to be dealt with by the police. But police measures are not enough. Any intelligent and experienced administrator of the criminal law will tell you that there are people who come up for punishment again and again for the same offence, and that punishing them is a cruel waste of time. There should be an Inquisition always available to consider whether these human nuisances should not be put out of their pain, or out of their joy as the case may be. The community must drive a much harder bargain for the privilege of citizenship than it now does; but it must also make the bargain not only practicable but in effect much easier than the present very imperfect bargain. This involves a new social creed. A new social creed involves a new heresy. A new heresy involves an Inquisition. The precedents established by the Inquisition furnish the material for a new legal code. Codification enables the work of the Inquisition to be done by an ordinary court of law. Thereupon the Inquisition, as such, disappears, precisely as the Tcheka has disappeared. Thus it has always been; and thus it ever shall be.

The moral of the dramatic fable of The Simpleton is now clear enough. With amateur Inquisitions under one name or another or no name at work in all directions, from Fascist *autos-da-fé* to American Vigilance Committees with lynching mobs as torturers and executioners, it is time for us to reconsider our Visions of Judgment, and see whether we cannot change them from old stories in which we no longer believe and new stories which are only too horribly true to serious and responsible public tribunals.

By the way, I had better guard myself against the assumption that because I have introduced into my fable a eugenic experiment in group marriage I am advocating the immediate adoption of that method of peopling the world for immediate practice by my readers. Group marriage is a form of marriage like any other; and it is just as well to remind our western and very insular Imperialists that marriage in the British Empire is startlingly different in the east from marriage in the British Isles; but I have introduced it only to bring into the story the four lovely phantasms who embody all the artistic, romantic, and military ideals of our cultured suburbs. On the Day of Judgment not merely do they cease to exist like the useless and predatory people: it becomes apparent that they never did exist. And, enchanting as they may be to our perfumers, who give us the concentrated odor of the flower without the roots or the clay or even the leaves, let us hope they never will.

On the Indian Ocean,
   April 1935.

The first performance of The Simpleton in England took place on the 29th July at the Malvern Festival of 1935 when the parts (in order of their appearance) were played by Godfrey Kenton, Arthur Ridley, Eileen Beldon, Derek Prentice, Cecil Trouncer, Vivienne Bennett, Elspeth Duxbury, Julian D'Albie, Stephen Murray, Donald Eccles, Norris Stayton, Curigwen Lewis, Elspeth March, and Richard Lonscale.

THE SIMPLETON OF
THE UNEXPECTED ISLES

PROLOGUE

The emigration office at a tropical port in the British Empire. The office is an annex of the harbor and customs sheds on one side and of the railway station on the other. Placards direct passengers TO THE CUSTOMS and TO THE TRAINS *through the open doors right and left respectively. The emigration officer, an unsatisfactory young man of unhealthy habits, is sitting writing at his table in the middle of the room. His clerk is at a standing desk against the wall on the customs side. The officer wears tropical clothes, neither too tidy nor too clean. The clerk is in a shabby dark lounge suit.*

THE E. O. [*finishing his writing*] Is that the lot?

CLERK. It's the lot from the French ship; but there is that case standing over from the Liverpool one.

THE E. O. [*exasperated*] Now look here, Wilks. Are you the emigration officer here or am I? Did I tell you that that girl was to be sent back or did I not?

WILKS. Well, I thought—

THE E. O. What business had you to think? I told you she was to go back. I suppose she tipped you to let her come here and make a scene on the chance of getting round me.

WILKS [*hotly*] Youll either take that back or prove it.

THE E. O. I will neither take it back nor prove it until you explain why you are letting this girl bother me again, though she has no papers, no passports, and is in excess of the quota without any excuse for it.

WILKS. Who's letting her bother you again? She told the High Commissioner that you had turned her down; and he told her she had better see you again.

THE E. O. And why the devil didnt you tell me that at first, instead of blithering about her as if she was a common case?

WILKS. The High Commissioner's daughter was on the ship

coming back from school. He came down to meet her. This girl had made friends with her or taken care of her or something.

THE E. O. Thats no good. We cant let her through on that.

WILKS. Well, will you see her?

THE E. O. Is she waiting to see me?

WILKS. She says she's waiting to see what will happen to her.

THE E. O. Same thing, isnt it?

WILKS. I suppose so. But she put it as if there was a difference. I think she's a bit mad. But the Medical Officer says she passes all his tests of sanity, though I could see that he has his doubts.

THE E. O. Oh, shut up. You need a medical test yourself, I think. Fetch her in.

Wilks goes out sulkily through the customs door and returns with a young woman. He leads her to the table and then goes back to his desk.

THE Y. W. Good morning, sir. You dont look as well as you did yesterday. Did you stay up too late?

THE E. O. [*nonplussed for the moment*] I— er— [*Collecting himself*] Look here, young lady. You have to answer questions here, not to ask them.

THE Y. W. You have been drinking.

THE E. O. [*springing up*] What the hell do you mean?

THE Y. W. You have. I smell it.

THE E. O. Very well. Back you go by the next boat, my lady.

THE Y. W. [*unmoved*] At this hour of the morning too! Dont you know you shouldnt?

THE E. O. [*to Wilks*] Take her away, you. [*To the young woman*] Out you go.

THE Y. W. I ought to speak to somebody about it. And look at the state the office is in! Whose business is it to see that it's properly dusted? Let me talk to them for you.

THE E. O. What concern is it of yours?

THE Y. W. I hate to see dust lying about. Look! You could write your name in it. And it's just awful to see a young man drinking before eleven in the morning.

WILKS [*propitiatory*] Dont say anything about it, Miss: I will see to the dust. Everybody starts the day with a drink here. Dont go talking, Miss, will you?

THE E. O. [*suddenly breaking down in tears*] You can go and tell who you damn well please. For two pins I'd chuck myself into the harbor and have done with it. This climate is hell: you cant stand it unless you drink till you see blue monkeys.

WILKS. Never mind him, Miss: he has nerves. We all have them here sooner or later, off and on. Here! I'll give you a landing ticket; and you just clear off and say nothing. [*He takes a ticket from the table and gives it to her*].

THE E. O. [*weeping*] A man's a slave here worse than a nigger. Spied on, reported on, checked and told off til he's afraid to have a pound note in his pocket or take a glass in his hand for fear of being had up for bribery or drinking. I'm fed up with it. Go and report me and be damned to you: what do I care? [*He sniffs and blows his nose, relieved by his outburst*].

WILKS. Would you have the kindness to clear out, Miss. We're busy. Youre passed all right: nothing to do but shew the ticket. You wont have to go back: we was only joking.

THE Y. W. But I want to go back. If this place is what he says, it is no place for me. And I did so enjoy the voyage out: I ask nothing better than to begin it all over again.

THE E. O. [*with the calm of despair*] Let her have her own way, Wilks. Shew her the way to the ship and shew her the way to the dock gate. She can take which she pleases. But get her out of this or I shall commit suicide.

THE Y. W. Why? Arnt you happy? It's not natural not to be happy. I'd be ashamed not to be happy.

THE E. O. What is there to make a man happy here?

THE Y. W. But you dont need to be made happy. You ought to be happy from the inside. Then you wouldnt need things to make you happy.

THE E. O. My inside! Oh Lord!

THE Y. W. Well, you can make your inside all right if you eat properly and stop drinking and keep the office dusted and your nice white clothes clean and tidy. You two are a disgrace.

THE E. O. [*roaring with rage*] Chuck that woman out.

WILKS. Chuck her yourself. What can *I* do? [*Imploringly to her*] If youd only have the goodness to go, Miss. We're so busy this morning.

THE Y. W. But I am a stranger here: I have nobody else to talk to. And you have nothing to do until the next boat comes in.

THE E. O. The next boat is due the day after tomorrow at five in the afternoon. Do you expect us to sit here talking to you until then?

THE Y. W. Well, it's I who have to do most of the talking, isnt it? Couldnt you shew me round the town? I'll pay for the taxi.

THE E. O. [*feebly rebellious*] Look here: you cant go on like this, you know.

THE Y. W. What were you going to do with yourself this morning if I hadnt come?

THE E. O. I—I—Whats that to you?

THE Y. W. I see you hadnt made up your mind. Let me make it up for you. Put on your hat and come along and shew me round. I seem to spend my life making up other people's minds for them.

THE E. O. [*helplessly*] All right, all right, all right. You neednt make a ballyhoo about it. But I ask myself—

THE Y. W. Dont ask yourself anything, my child. Let life come to you. March.

THE E. O. [*at the railway door, to Wilks, in a last effort to assert himself*] Carry on, you. [*He goes*].

THE Y. W. Wouldnt you like to come too?

WILKS. Yes, Miss; but somebody must stay in the office; and it had better be me than him. I am indispensable.

THE Y. W. What a word! Dispensables and indispensables: there you have the whole world. I wonder am I a dispensable or an indispensable. [*She goes out through the railway door*].

WILKS [*alone*] Let life come to you. Sounds all right, that. Let life come to you. Aye; but suppose life doesnt come to you! Look at me! What am I? An empire builder: thats what I am by nature. Cecil Rhodes: thats me. Why am I a clerk with only

two shirts to my back, with that young waster wiping his dirty
boots on me for doing the work he cant do himself, though he
gets all the praise and all the pudding? Because life never came
to me like it came to Rhodes. Found his backyard full of
diamonds, he did; and nothing to do but wash the clay off them
and be a millionaire. I had Rhodes's idea all right. Let the whole
earth be England, I said to the school teacher; and let Englishmen govern it. Nobody put that into my head: it came of itself.
But what did I find in my backyard? Next door's dead cat. Could
I make myself head of a Chartered Company with a dead cat?
And when I threw it back over the wall my mother said "You
have thrown away your luck, my boy" she says "you shouldnt
have thrown it back: you should have passed it on, like a chain
letter. Now you will never have no more luck in this world."
And no more I have. I says to her "I'll be in the papers yet some
day" I says "like Cecil Rhodes: you see if I'm not." "Not you,
my lad" she says. "Everything what comes to you you throw it
back." Well, so I do. Look at this girl here. "Come with me" she
says. And I threw the cat back again. "Somebody must be left
in the office" I says. "I am indispensable" I says. And all the
time I knew that nobody neednt be in the office, and that any
Jew boy could do all I do here and do it better. But I promised
my mother I'd get into the papers; and I will. I have that much
of the Rhodes touch in me. [*He sits at the table and writes on a
luggage label; then reads what he has written*] "Here lies a man
who might have been Cecil Rhodes if he had had Rhodes's luck.
Mother, farewell: your son has kept his word." [*He ties the label
to the lapel of his coat*] Wheres that fool's gun? [*He opens a
drawer and takes out a brandy flask and an automatic pistol, which
he throws on the table*]. I'll damned well shew em whether I'm an
empire builder or not. That lassie shant say that I didnt leave
the place tidy either, though she can write in the dust of it with
her finger. [*He shuts the drawer, and places the chair trimly at the
table. Then he goes to his desk and takes out a duster, with which
he wipes first the desk and then the table. He replaces the duster in
the desk, and takes out a comb and a hand mirror. He tidies his hair;*

23

replaces the comb and glass in the desk; closes it and sets the stool in its place before it. He then returns to the table, and empties the flask at a draught]. Now for it. The back of the head: thats the Russian touch. [*He takes the pistol and presents it over his shoulder to his occiput*]. Let the whole earth be England; and let Englishmen rule it. [*Singing*] Rule Britannia: Britannia rules the wa—

He blows his brains out and falls dead. The Station Master enters.

THE STATION MASTER. Here! Who's been shooting here? [*He sees the body*] Wilks!! Dear! dear! dear! What a climate! The fifth this month. [*He goes to the door*]. Hallo there, Jo. Bring along the stretcher and two or three with you. Mr Wilks has shot himself.

JO [*without, cheerfully*] Right you are, sir.

THE STATION MASTER. What a climate! Poor old Wilks!

SCENE II

A grassy cliff top overhanging the sea. A seat for promenaders. The young woman and the emigration officer stand on the brink.

THE Y. W. Pity theres no beach. We could bathe.

THE E. O. Not us. Not likely. Theres sharks there. And killer whales, worse than any sharks.

THE Y. W. It looks pretty deep.

THE E. O. I should think it is. The biggest liners can get close up. Like Plymouth. Like Lulworth Cove. Dont stand so close. Theres a sort of fascination in it; and you might get giddy.

They come away from the edge and sit on the seat together: she on his left, he nearest the sea.

THE Y. W. It's lovely here. Better than the town.

THE E. O. Dont deceive yourself. It's a horrible place. The climate is something terrible. Do you know that if you hadnt come in this morning I'd have done myself in.

THE Y. W. Dont talk nonsense. Why should you do yourself in?

THE E. O. Yes I should. I had the gun ready in the drawer of that table. I'd have shot Wilks and then shot myself.

THE Y. W. Why should you shoot poor Wilks? What has he

24

done?

THE E. O. I hate him. He hates me. Everybody here hates everybody else. And the fellow is so confoundedly smug and happy and satisfied: it drives me mad when I can hardly bear my own life. No fear of him shooting himself: not much. So I thought I'd save him the trouble.

THE Y. W. But that would be murder.

THE E. O. Not if I shot myself after. That would make us quits.

THE Y. W. Well, I am surprised to hear a young man like you, in the prime of life as you might say, talking like that. Why dont you get married?

THE E. O. My salary's too small for a white woman. Theyre all snobs; and they want a husband only to take them home out of this.

THE Y. W. Why, it's an earthly paradise.

THE E. O. Tell them so; and see what theyll say to you.

THE Y. W. Well, why not marry a colored woman?

THE E. O. You dont know what youre talking about. Ive tried. But now theyre all educated they wont look at a white man. They tell me I'm ignorant and that I smell bad.

THE Y. W. Well, so you do. You smell of drink and indigestion and sweaty clothes. You were quite disgusting when you tried to make up to me in the taxi. Thats why I got out, and made for the sea air.

THE E. O. [*rising hurriedly*] I cant stand any more of this. [*He takes a wallet of papers from his breast pocket and throws them on the seat*]. Hand them in at the office, will you: theyll be wanted there. I am going over.

He makes for the edge of the cliff. But there is a path down the cliff face, invisible from the seat. A native priest, a handsome man in the prime of life, beautifully dressed, rises into view by this path and bars his way.

PRIEST. Pardon, son of empire. This cliff contains the temple of the goddess who is beyond naming, the eternal mother, the seed and the sun, the resurrection and the life. You must not die here. I will send an acolyte to guide you to the cliff of death, which contains the temple of the goddess's brother, the weeder of the garden, the sacred scavenger, the last friend on earth, the prolonger of sleep and the giver of rest. It is not far off: life and death dwell close together: you need prolong your unhappiness only a bare five minutes. The priest there will attend to your remains and see they are disposed of with all becoming rites.

THE E. O. [*to the young woman*] Is he real; or is it the drink?

THE Y. W. He's real. And, my word! isnt he jolly good looking? [*To the priest*] Youll excuse this young man, sir, wont you? He's been drinking pretty hard.

THE PRIEST [*advancing between them*] Blame him not, sweet one. He comes from a strange mad country where the young are taught languages that are dead and histories that are lies, but are never told how to eat and drink and clothe themselves and reproduce their species. They worship strange ancient gods; and they play games with balls marvellously well; but of the great game of life they are ignorant. Here, where they are in the midst of life and loveliness, they die by their own hands to escape what they call the horrors. We do not encourage them to live. The empire is for those who can live in it, not for those who can only die in it. Take your friend to the cliff of death; and bid him farewell tenderly; for he is very unhappy.

THE E. O. Look here: I am an Englishman; and I shall commit suicide where I please. No nigger alive shall dictate to me.

THE PRIEST. It is forbidden.

THE E. O. Who's to stop me? Will you?

The priest shakes his head and makes way for him.

THE Y. W. Oh, you are not going to let him do it, are you?

THE PRIEST [*holding her back*] We never offer violence to the unhappy. Do not interfere with his destiny.

THE E. O. [*planting himself on the edge and facing the abyss*] I am going to do it: see? Nobody shall say that I lived a dog's life because I was afraid to make an end of it. [*He bends his knees to spring, but cannot*]. I WILL. [*He makes another effort, bending almost to his haunches, but again fails to make the spring-up a spring-over*].

THE PRIEST. Poor fellow! Let me assist you. [*He shoots his foot against the E. O.'s posterior and sends him over the cliff*].

THE E. O. [*in a tone of the strongest remonstrance as he is catapulted into the void*] Oh! [*A prodigious splash*].

THE Y. W. Murderer!

THE PRIEST. Not quite. There are nets below, and a palisade to keep out the sharks. The shock will do him good.

THE Y. W. Well, I never!

THE PRIEST. Come, young rose blossom, and feast with us in the temple.

THE Y. W. Not so much rose blossom, young man. Are there any priestesses down there?

THE PRIEST. Of course. How can men feast without women?

THE Y. W. Well, let life come to you I always say; and dont cry out until youre hurt. After you, sir.

They descend.

SCENE III

A shelf of rock half way down the cliff forms an esplanade between the sea and a series of gigantic images of oriental deities in shallow alcoves cut in the face of the wall of rock. A feast of fruit and bread and soft drinks is spread on the ground. The young woman is sitting at it between the priest on her right nearest the sea and a very handsome young native priestess in robes of dusky yellow silk on her left nearest the images.

THE Y. W. You know, to me this is a funny sort of lunch. You begin with the dessert. We begin with the entrées. I suppose it's all right; but I have eaten so much fruit and bread and stuff that I dont feel I want any meat.

THE PRIEST. We shall not offer you any. We dont eat it.

THE Y. W. Then how do you keep up your strength?

THE PRIEST. It keeps itself up.

THE Y. W. Oh, how could that be? [*To the priestess*] You wouldnt like a husband that didnt eat plenty of meat, would you? But then youre a priestess; so I suppose it doesnt matter to you, as you cant marry.

27

THE PRIESTESS. I am married.

THE Y. W. Oh! And you a priestess!

THE PRIESTESS. I could not be a priestess if I were not married. How could I presume to teach others without a completed human experience? How could I deal with children if I were not a mother?

THE Y. W. But that isnt right. My sister was a teacher; but when she married they took her job away from her and wouldnt let her teach any more.

THE PRIESTESS. The rulers of your country must be mad.

THE Y. W. Oh no. Theyre all right: just like other people. [*To the priest*] I say, reverend. What about the poor lad you kicked over the cliff? Is he really safe? I dont feel easy about him.

THE PRIEST. His clothes are drying in the sun. They will lend him some clothes and send him up here as soon as he has recovered from his ducking.

An English lady tourist, Baedeker in hand, has wandered in, trying to identify the images with the aid of her book. She now comes behind the seated group and accosts the priest.

THE L. T. Excuse me; but can you tell me which of these figures is the principal god?

THE PRIEST [*rising courteously*] The principal one? I do not understand.

THE L. T. I get lost among all these different gods: it is so difficult to know which is which.

THE PRIEST. They are not different gods. They are all god.

THE L. T. But how can that be? The figures are different.

THE PRIEST. God has many aspects.

THE L. T. But all these names in the guide book?

THE PRIEST. God has many names.

THE L. T. Not with us, you know.

THE PRIEST. Yes: even with you. The Father, the Son, the Spirit, the Immaculate Mother—

THE L. T. Excuse me. We are not Catholics.

THE PRIESTESS [*sharply*] Are your temples then labelled "For men only"?

THE L. T. [*shocked*] Oh, really! So sorry to have troubled you. [*She hurries away*].

THE PRIEST [*resuming his seat*] You should not be rude to the poor lady. She is English, and doesnt understand.

THE PRIESTESS. I find these heathen idolaters very trying. Is it really kind to treat them according to their folly instead of to our wisdom?

THE Y. W. Here! Steady on, you. Who are you calling heathen idolaters? Look at all those images. I should say, if you ask me, that the boot is on the other leg.

THE PRIEST. Those images are not idols: they are personifications of the forces of nature by which we all live. But of course to an idolater they are idols.

THE Y. W. You talk a lot about religion here. Cant you think of something livelier? I always say let life come to you; and dont bother about religion.

THE PRIESTESS. An excellent rule. But the more you let life come to you, the more you will find yourself bothering about religion.

The Emigration Officer rises into view in a spotless white robe. He is clean and rather pale, but looks regenerated.

THE Y. W. Oh boy, you do look the better for your dip. Why, he's an angel, a lamb. What have you done to him?

THE E. O. [*seating himself at the end of the table with his back to the sea*] Well, if you want to know, this blighter kicked me into the sea; and when I'd swallowed a ton or two of your best salt water they fished me out in a net and emptied me out. I brought up my immortal soul. They gave me what I thought was a nice cup of their tea to settle my stomach; but it made me ten times as sick as I was before. Theres nothing of the man you met this morning left except his skin and bones. You may regard me as to all intents and purposes born again.

THE PRIEST. Do you still wish to kill yourself?

THE E. O. When you have been through what I have been through since they fished me out of the water you wont worry about trifles as I used to, old man.

THE Y. W. Thats right. Let life come to you, I always say.

THE E. O. Yes, let life come. The premises are quite empty.

THE LADY TOURIST [*returning and addressing the priest*] Excuse me; but I have been thinking so much about you since you spoke to me. Would you mind accepting and reading this little tract?

THE PRIEST [*rising and coming forward to her, meanwhile reading the title with a polite show of interest*] "Where will you spend eternity?"

THE L. T. [*strangely moved*] I have been haunted by your face. I could not bear to think of your spending eternity in torment. I feel sure it is a Christian face.

THE PRIEST. It is very kind of you. I will read the tract with the greatest attention. Thank you.

The lady, having no excuse for staying, moves away reluctantly towards the images.

THE PRIESTESS [*calling after her imperiously*] Where have you spent eternity so far, may I ask? That which has no end can have no beginning?

THE L. T. Excuse me: I have no desire to speak to you.

THE Y. W. [*indicating the priest*] Fallen in love with him, have you? Well, let yourself rip. Let life come to you.

THE L. T. Oh! How dare you? Really! Really!! [*She goes out indignantly*].

THE PRIESTESS. Another conquest, Pra?

THE Y. W. Is his name Pra?

THE PRIESTESS. He has many names; but he answers to Pra when you call him.

THE Y. W. Oh, what a way to put it! The man isnt a dog, is he?

THE PRIESTESS. He inspires a doglike devotion in women. He once did in me; so I know.

THE PRIEST. Dont be vindictive, Prola. I dont do it on purpose. [*He sits down again, this time next her on her left*].

THE PRIESTESS. No: you do it by instinct. That, also, is rather doglike.

THE PRIEST. No matter: I shall soon get the poor lady beyond the doglike stage.

THE E. O. [*who has been unable to take his eyes off the priestess*] Is your name Prola?

THE PRIEST. She has many names: some of them terrible ones; but she answers to Prola when you call her.

THE PRIESTESS. Young man: are my eyes like the fishpools of Heshbon?

THE E. O. Well, I have never seen the fishpools of Heshbon; but your eyes make me feel like that.

THE Y. W. Seems to me theres some sort of magic about this old cave thats dangerous. If you dont mind, I'll bid you all good morning. I always say let life come to you; but here it's coming a bit too thick for me. [*She rises*].

THE PRIESTESS. Wait. We can share him.

THE Y. W. Well I never! [*She flops back into her seat, flabbergasted*].

THE PRIESTESS. Hush. Look.

The Lady Tourist returns and again goes to the priest.

THE L. T. Excuse me; but could I have a word with you alone?

THE PRIEST [*rising*] Certainly. Come with me.

They go into the caves together.

THE E. O. What about a word with me alone, Prola?

THE Y. W. [*with redoubled emphasis*] Well I NEVER!!

THE PRIESTESS [*to the Officer*] You are not yet sufficiently regenerated. But you may hope.

THE Y. W. You take care, boy. I think youve got a touch of the sun. You cant be too careful in the tropics.

An English male tourist enters from among the images. He is on the young side of middle age, with pleasant aristocratic appearance and manners.

THE M. T. Excuse me: I have mislaid my wife. English lady with a guide book. Wears glasses. Bi-focals.

THE Y. W. Her husband! Oh, I say!

THE E. O. [*rising deferentially*] Just left us, Sir Charles.

THE M. T. Hallo! Weve met before, I think, havnt we?

THE E. O. When you landed, Sir Charles. I am the emigration officer.

SIR CHARLES. Ah, of course: yes. You know Lady Farwaters by sight. Which way did she go?

THE E. O. I am sorry: I didnt notice.

SIR CHARLES [*worried*] I wonder what she can be doing.

THE Y. W. So do I.

SIR CHARLES. I beg your pardon?

THE Y. W. Granted.

THE PRIESTESS [*rising and coming to him*] May I shew you round the temple, Sir Charles? We shall probably find her there.

SIR CHARLES [*who has not yet hitherto looked particularly at her*] No thank you, no, no.

THE PRIESTESS. It is interesting. I am not a professional guide: I am a priestess; and I will see that you are not asked for anything. You had better come with me.

SIR CHARLES. No: I— [*he looks at her. His tone changes instantly*]. Well, yes, if you will be so good. Certainly. Thank you. *They go into the alcoves together.*

THE Y. W. [*leaving the table*] Oh boy, what do you think of this abode of love? Lady Farwaters, as white as Canterbury veal, has fallen for a brown bishop; and her husband, the whitest English west-end white, has been carried off to her den by an amber colored snake charmer. Lets get out of it while we're safe.

THE E. O. I feel quite safe, thank you. I have been cleaned up. You havnt.

THE Y. W. What do you mean, I havnt?

THE E. O. I mean that you were quite right to object to me half an hour ago. Your offensive personal remarks were fully justified. But now the tables are turned. I havnt gone through the fire; but Ive gone through the water. And the water has gone through me. It is for me now to object and to make personal remarks.

THE Y. W. Make as much as one; and you will get your face smacked.

THE E. O. [*seizing her by the wrist and the back of her collar*] Go and get cleaned up, you disgusting little devil. [*He rushes her to the edge*].

THE Y. W. [*screaming*] No.

THE E. O. Yes. [*He hurls her over*].

A scream cut short by a splash. The E. O. sits down at the table and attacks the remains of the feast ravenously.

THE PROLOGUE ENDS

D

ACT I

The lawn of a stately house on the north coast of a tropical island in the Pacific commands a fine view of the ocean and of a breakwater enclosing a harbor, large enough to accommodate a fleet, but at present shipless. The western face of the house is reached by a terrace and a flight of steps. The steps lead down to a crescent formed by two curved stone seats separated by a patch of sward surrounding a circular well with a low marble parapet. This parapet, like the stone seats, has silk cushions scattered about it.

Behind the crescent the lawn is banked to a higher level and becomes a flower garden, sheltered from the wind by shrubberies. To the west of the flower garden the lawn falls away to the sea, but not to sea level, all that is visible of the port being the top of the light-house. There are trees enough in all directions to provide shade everywhere.

However, the raised flower garden is the centre of interest; for in it are four shrines marking the corners of a square. In the two foremost shrines two girl-goddesses sit crosslegged. In the two further ones two youthful gods are sitting in the same fashion. The ages of the four appear to be between 17 and 20. They are magically beautiful in their Indian dresses, softly brilliant, making the tropical flowers of the garden seem almost crude beside them. Their expressions are intent, grave, and inscrutable. They face south with their backs to the sea. The goddess to the east has raven black hair, a swarthy skin, and robes of a thousand shades of deep carnation, in contrast to the younger one on her right, who is a ravishing blonde in a diaphanous white and gold sari. There is a parallel contrast between the two youths, the one on the west being the younger and more delicate, and the one on his left older and more powerfully framed.

The four figures give the garden a hieratic aspect which has its effect on a young English clergyman, who wanders into the grounds at the north west corner, looking curiously and apprehensively about him with the air of a stranger who is trespassing. When he catches sight of the four figures he starts nervously and whips off his hat;

34

then approaches them on tiptoe. He has a baby complexion, and a childish expression, credulous and disarmingly propitiatory. His age is at most 24.

Down the steps at this moment comes Pra, about twenty years older than when we saw him last, but splendidly preserved. His approach is dignified and even courteous, though not warmly so. He evidently wants to know what the stranger is doing in his garden.

THE CLERGYMAN [*nervously, hat in hand*] I beg your pardon. I fear I am trespassing. I am a stranger here; and I could not find a road up from the beach. I thought I might cut across through your grounds. [*Indicating the figures*] But I assure you I had no idea I was intruding on consecrated ground.

PRA. You are not on consecrated ground, except in so far as all ground is consecrated.

THE CLERGYMAN. Oh, excuse me. I thought—those idols—

PRA. Idols!

THE CLERGYMAN. No, of course not idols. I meant those gods and goddesses—

PRA. They are very beautiful, are they not? [*He speaks without awe or enthusiasm, with a touch of pity for the parson and weariness on his own part*].

THE CLERGYMAN. They are most beautiful. Quite marvellous even to me, an English clergyman. I can hardly wonder at your worshipping them, though of course you shouldnt.

PRA. Beauty is worshipful, within limits. When you have worshipped your fill may I shew you the shortest way out? It is through the house. Where do you wish to go, by the way?

THE CLERGYMAN. I dont know. I am lost.

PRA. Lost?

THE CLERGYMAN. Yes, quite lost. I dont know where I am. I mean I dont even know what country I am in.

PRA. You are in the Unexpected Isles, a Crown Colony of the British Empire.

THE CLERGYMAN. Do you mean the isles that came up out of the sea when I was a baby.

PRA. Yes. [*Pointing to the breakwater*] That is the harbor of the

35

port of Good Adventure.

THE CLERGYMAN. They put me on shore there.

PRA. Who put you on shore?

THE CLERGYMAN. The pirates.

PRA. Pirates!

THE CLERGYMAN. Yes. I was their chaplain.

PRA. You were their—! [*He turns to the house and calls*] Prola. Prola.

PROLA'S VOICE. Yes. What is it?

PRA. Come out here.

Prola comes down the steps. She, like Pra, is twenty years older; but the years have only made her beauty more impressive.

THE CLERGYMAN [*gaping at her in undisguised awe and admiration*] Oh dear! Is this the lady of the house?

PROLA [*coming past Pra to the Clergyman*] Who is this gentleman?

PRA. He does not seem to know. I think he has escaped from the asylum.

THE CLERGYMAN [*distressed*] Oh, dear beautiful lady, I am not mad. Everybody thinks I am. Nobody believes what I say, though it is the simple truth. I know it is very hard to believe.

PROLA. In the Unexpected Isles nothing is unbelievable. How did you get in here?

THE CLERGYMAN. I lost my way trying to find a short cut up from the beach. I climbed the fence. I am so sorry.

PROLA. Really sorry?

THE CLERGYMAN. I did not mean to intrude. I apologize most sincerely.

PROLA. I did not ask you to apologize: you are quite welcome. I asked were you really sorry. Do you regret finding yourself in this garden?

THE CLERGYMAN. Oh no. It's like the Garden of Eden: I should like to stay here forever. [*Suddenly breaking down to the verge of tears*] I have nowhere to go.

PROLA. Perhaps he is weak with hunger.

THE CLERGYMAN. No: it's not that. I have been under a great

strain for a long time; and now that I have escaped—and the beauty of those four—and your lovely awfulness—and—oh [*collapsing on the stone seat*] I am making a fool of myself. I always make a fool of myself. Dont mind me.

PRA. He thinks he has been chaplain in a pirate ship.

THE CLERGYMAN [*rising in desperate protest*] But I have. I have. They kidnapped me at Weston Super Mare where I was doing locum tenens for the Rector of Saint Biddulphs. It was on a Sunday afternoon: I had my clerical clothes on after taking the afternoon service. "You look so innocent and respectable" they said. "Just what we want!" They took me all over the world, where I couldnt speak the language and couldnt explain.

PRA. And they wanted you to minister to them spiritually?

THE CLERGYMAN. No no: that was what was so dreadful. They were crooks, racketeers, smugglers, pirates, anything that paid them. They used me to make people believe that they were respectable. They were often so bored that they made me hold a service and preach; but it was only to make themselves ill laughing at me. Though perhaps I shouldnt say that. Some of them were such dear nice fellows: they assured me it did them no end of good. But they got tired of me and put me ashore here. [*He again resorts to the stone seat, clasping his temples distractedly*] Oh dear! oh dear! nothing ever happens to me that happens to other people. And all because I was not a natural baby. I was a nitrogen baby.

PROLA. A nitrogen baby!

PRA [*to Prola*] Steady. There may be something in this. [*He goes to the clergyman and sits down beside him*] What do you mean by a nitrogen baby?

THE CLERGYMAN. You see, my father is a famous biological chemist.

PROLA. I do not see. Your father may be a biological chemist; but biological chemists' children are like other people's children.

THE CLERGYMAN. No. No, I assure you. Not my father's children. You dont know my father. Even my Christian name is Phosphor.

PRA. Is what?

THE CLERGYMAN. Phosphor. [*He spells it*] P.H.O.S.P.H.O.R. The name of the morning star. Phosphorus, you know. The stuff they make matches with. Such a name to baptize a boy by! Please dont call me by it.

PRA. Come come! Neither your father nor your godfathers and godmothers could change your human nature by giving you an unusual name in baptism.

THE CLERGYMAN. But it wasnt only the name. My father fed our cows on nitrogen grass.

PRA. Nitrogen gas, you mean.

THE CLERGYMAN. No: nitrogen grass. Some sort of grass that came up when he sprinkled our fields with chemicals. The cows ate it; and their butter was very yellow and awfully rich. So was the milk. I was fed on that sort of milk and butter. And the wheat in my bread was grown from special nitrates that my father made.

PRA [*to Prola*] I believe he is not mad after all.

THE CLERGYMAN. I assure you I am not. I am weakminded; but I am not mad.

PRA. I have read some very interesting articles about this by an English chemist named Hammingtap.

THE CLERGYMAN. Thats my father. My name is Hammingtap. The old family name is Hummingtop; but my grandfather changed it when he was at Oxford.

PRA. Prola: our young friend here may really be a new sort of man. Shall we go in and tell the others about him? We might take him into the family for a while, as an experiment.

THE CLERGYMAN [*alarmed*] Oh please, no. Why does everyone want to make an experiment of me?

PROLA. All men and women are experiments. What is your religion?

THE CLERGYMAN. The Christian religion, of course. I am a clergyman.

PROLA. What is the Christian religion?

THE CLERGYMAN. Well, it is—well, I suppose it is the Christian

38

religion. I thought everybody knew. But then of course you are a heathen.

PROLA. What does the Christian religion mean to you?

THE CLERGYMAN. Oh, to me it means everything that is good and lovely and kind and holy. I dont profess to go any further than that.

PROLA. You need not. You had better not. Wait here until we return. We may find some use for you. Come, Pra.

She goes up the steps into the house, followed by Pra. The Clergyman, left with the four figures, looks at them, looks round to make sure that nobody is watching. Then he steals up to the fair goddess.

THE CLERGYMAN. Oh, how lovely you are! How I wish you were alive and I could kiss your living lips instead of the paint on a hard wooden image. I wonder is it idolatry to adore you? St Peter in Rome is only a bronze image; but his feet have been worn away by the kisses of Christian pilgrims. You make me feel as I have never felt before. I must kiss you. [*He does so and finds that she is alive. She smiles as her eyes turn bewitchingly towards him*]. Oh!!! [*He stands gasping, palpitating*].

THE ELDER YOUTH. Beware.

THE YOUNGER. On guard.

THE FAIR GIRL. Let him worship. His lips are sweet and pure.

THE DARK ONE. "For he on honey dew hath fed"—

THE FAIR ONE.—"and drunk the milk of paradise."

THE DARK ONE. I, Vashti, can see his aura. It is violet.

THE FAIR ONE. I, Maya, can see his halo. It is silvery.

VASHTI. Blessed are the shining ones!

MAYA. Blessed are the simple ones!

THE ELDER YOUTH. Beware. I, Janga, warn thee.

THE YOUNGER YOUTH. On guard. I, Kanchin, shew thee the red light.

JANGA. Their eyebrows are drawn bows.

KANCHIN. Their arrows feel sweet in the heart—

JANGA. —but are deadly.

KANCHIN. The ground within reach of their arms is enchanted.

JANGA. Vashti is lovely even to her brothers.

KANCHIN. Little children would die for Maya.

JANGA. Beware.

KANCHIN. On guard.

JANGA. Trust them not.

KANCHIN. They will break thy spear.

JANGA. They will pierce thy shield.

VASHTI. Fear not, beginner: I will strengthen thee.

MAYA. Strive not, beloved: I will keep thy soul for thee.

THE 2 YOUTHS [*together, fortissimo*] Beware.

The two girl-goddesses suddenly and simultaneously spring from their shrines and march down upon him, Vashti to his left, Maya to his right.

VASHTI. Dare you tread the plains of heaven with us, young pilgrim?

MAYA. We are waves of life in a sea of bliss. Dare you breast them, young swimmer?

THE CLERGYMAN. Oh, I dont know whether you are gods and goddesses or real people. I only know that you fill my heart with inexpressible longings.

MAYA. We are the awakening.

VASHTI. We are the way.

MAYA. We are the life.

VASHTI. I am the light. Look at me. [*She throws her arm round him and turns his face to hers*].

MAYA. I am the fire. Feel how it glows [*She also throws her arm round him*].

LADY FARWATERS *comes from the house, and pauses at the top of the steps to take in what is going on.*

THE CLERGYMAN. Oh, one at a time, please.

VASHTI. Perfect love casteth out choice.

MAYA. In love there is neither division nor measure.

LADY FARWATERS [*rushing to him and dragging him away from them*] Stop it, children: you are driving the man mad. Go away, all of you.

The two youths spring from their pedestals and whirl the girls away through the shrubberies.

40

VASHTI [*invisible, calling*] I will return in dreams.

MAYA [*similarly*] I leave my arrow in your heart.

LADY FARWATERS. You mustnt mind them.

Prola and Pra come down the steps, followed by Sir Charles Farwaters and by Hugo Hyering C.B. and Mrs Hyering. Hyering is the former emigration officer, now an elderly and very different man, disciplined, responsible and well groomed. His wife is the emigrant girl twenty years older and better drilled socially, but still very much her old self. Lady Farwaters, once a gaunt and affected tourist visiting cave temples and distributing tracts to the heathen, is now a bland and attractive matron.

PRA. Mr Hammingtap: let me introduce you to the Governor of the Unexpected Isles, Sir Charles Farwaters.

SIR CHARLES [*offering his hand*] How do you do, Mr Hammingtap?

THE CLERGYMAN [*jerkily nervous*] Very pleased. [*They shake hands*].

Sir Charles sits down in the middle of the stone seat nearest the steps.

PRA. Lady Farwaters.

LADY FARWATERS [*smiles and proffers her hand*]!

THE CLERGYMAN. Most kind— er. [*He shakes*].

Lady Farwaters sits down in the middle of the other stone seat.

PRA. This is Mr Hugo Hyering, political secretary to the Isles.

THE CLERGYMAN. How do you do, Sir Hugo?

HYERING [*shaking hands*] Not Sir Hugo. [*Introducing*] Mrs Hyering.

MRS HYERING [*shaking hands*] C.B., in case you are addressing a letter. [*She sits down on Sir Charles's left*].

THE CLERGYMAN. Oh, I am so sorry.

HYERING. Not at all. [*He sits on Lady Farwaters' right*].

PRA [*indicating the parapet of the well*] You had better sit here.

THE CLERGYMAN [*sitting down as directed*] Thank you.

Prola sits down on Sir Charles's left, and Pra on Lady Farwaters' left.

LADY FARWATERS. You have made the acquaintance of our

41

four children, Mr Hammingtap?

THE CLERGYMAN. I couldnt help it. I mean—

PROLA. We know what you mean. You need not explain.

THE CLERGYMAN. But I assure you I—that is—

MRS HYERING. Dont apologize, Mr Hammingtap. We know quite well what our daughters are capable of when they are attracted by a young stranger.

THE CLERGYMAN. I did not understand. They are so sunburnt, and their dresses are so eastern: I thought they were orientals.

SIR CHARLES. They are half orientals. You see, the family is a mixed one. This lady, whom you may address as Prola, and this gentleman, known as Pra, are both entirely oriental, and very dominant personalities at that; so that naturally our children would have a strong oriental strain, would they not?

THE CLERGYMAN [hastily] Oh, of course. Quite. Certainly. [He looks piteously at their gracious unconcerned faces, which tell him nothing]. I beg your pardon. I am frightfully sorry; but my nerves are in rags; and I cannot follow what you are saying.

HYERING. Oh yes you can. It's all right: you have understood perfectly.

MRS HYERING. Buck up, Mr Hammingtap. Let life come to you.

LADY FARWATERS. Our family arrangements are not those usual in England. We are making a little domestic experiment—

THE CLERGYMAN. Oh, not an experiment, I hope. Chemical experiments are bad enough: I am one myself; but they are scientific. I dont think I could countenance a domestic experiment. And in spite of what you say I am not sure that I am not going mad.

SIR CHARLES. We are distracting you. Let us change the subject. Would you like to be a bishop?

THE CLERGYMAN. Oh dear! Can you make me one?

SIR CHARLES. Well, my recommendation would probably be decisive. A bishop is needed here: a bishop in partibus infidelium. Providence seems to have thrown you on this shore for the purpose, like Jonah. Will you undertake it?

THE CLERGYMAN. I should like to have a bishop's salary, certainly. But unfortunately I am weakminded.

SIR CHARLES. Many bishops are; and they are the best sort. A strongminded bishop is a horror.

THE CLERGYMAN. I am too young.

SIR CHARLES. You will not remain so. Most bishops are too old.

THE CLERGYMAN [tempted] It would be rather a lark, wouldnt it?

MRS HYERING. Thats right, Mr Hammingtap: let life come to you.

PRA. What objection have you to be a bishop?

THE CLERGYMAN. Oh, none, I assure you. Of course no clergyman could object to be a bishop. But why do you want to make me one?

SIR CHARLES. I will be quite frank with you, Mr Hammingtap. Twenty years ago my wife and I, with Mr and Mrs Hyering, joined this eastern gentleman and his colleague in a eugenic experiment. Its object was to try out the result of a biological blend of the flesh and spirit of the west with the flesh and spirit of the east. We formed a family of six parents.

THE CLERGYMAN. Six?

SIR CHARLES. Yes, six. The result has been a little disappointing from the point of view of numbers; but we have produced four children, two of each sex, and educated them in the most enlightened manner we were capable of. They have now grown up; consequently the time has arrived when the family group must be extended by young persons of their own age, so that the group may produce a second generation. Now sooner or later this extension of the family group will set people talking.

THE CLERGYMAN. It would strike my people dumb, if I grasp your meaning rightly.

SIR CHARLES. You do. I mean exactly what I say. There will be a struggle with public opinion in the empire. We shall not shirk it: it is part of our plan to open people's minds on the subject of eugenics and the need for mixing not only western and eastern culture but eastern and western blood. Still, we do not want to be stopped, as the Mormons were, or as the Oneida

Community would have been if it had not voluntarily broken up. We want to set the intelligent people talking, and to strike the stupid people dumb. And we think we could do both by adding a bishop to the family.

MRS HYERING. And that is where you come in, young man.

PRA. There is another consideration that weighs with us: at least with me. I am convinced that there is something lacking in the constitution of the children. It may be a deficiency of nitrogen. It certainly is a deficiency of something that is essential to a complete social human being.

THE CLERGYMAN. Oh, I cannot believe that. They seemed to me to be quite perfect. I cannot imagine anyone more perfect than Maya.

PRA. Well, what did you think of Maya's conscience, for example?

THE CLERGYMAN [bewildered] Her conscience? I suppose—I dont know—I—

PRA. Precisely. You dont know. Well, we do know. Our four wonderful children have all sorts of talents, all sorts of accomplishments, all sorts of charms. And we are heartily tired of all their attractions because, though they have artistic consciences, and would die rather than do anything ugly or vulgar or common, they have not between the whole four of them a scrap of moral conscience. They have been very carefully fed: all the vitamins that the biological chemists have discovered are provided in their diet. All their glands are scientifically nourished. Their physical health is perfect. Unfortunately the biological chemists have not yet discovered either the gland that produces and regulates the moral conscience or the vitamins that nourish it. Have you a conscience, Mr Hammingtap?

THE CLERGYMAN. Oh yes: I wish I hadnt. It tortures me. You know, I should have enjoyed being a pirate's chaplain sometimes if it hadnt been for my terrible conscience. It has made my life one long remorse; for I have never had the strength of mind to act up to it.

PRA. That suggests very strongly that the conscientious man

44

is, chemically speaking, the nitrogenic man. Here, then, we have four young adults, insufficiently nitrogenized, and therefore deficient in conscience. Here also we have a young adult saturated with nitrogen from his cradle, and suffering from a morbid excess of conscience. A union between him and our girls is clearly indicated.

THE CLERGYMAN. You mean that I ought to marry one of them?

PRA. Not at all. They would regard that as an invidious proceeding.

THE CLERGYMAN. Invidious! I dont understand.

LADY FARWATERS [*goodnaturedly*] Let me try to break it to you, Mr Hammingtap. The two girls attract you very much, dont they?

THE CLERGYMAN. How can one help being attracted, Lady Farwaters? Theyre quite beautiful.

LADY FARWATERS. Both of them?

THE CLERGYMAN. Oh, as a clergyman I could not be attracted by more than one at a time. Still, somehow, I seem to love them all in an inexpressible sort of way. Only, if there were any question of marriage, I should have to choose.

PROLA. And which would you choose?

THE CLERGYMAN. Oh, I should choose Maya.

PROLA. Maya would at once reject you.

THE CLERGYMAN [*much dejected*] I suppose so. I know I am no catch for Maya. Still, she was very kind to me. In fact—but perhaps I oughtnt to tell you this—she kissed me.

SIR CHARLES. Indeed? That shews that she contemplates a union with you.

LADY FARWATERS. You must not think she would reject you on the ground of any personal unworthiness on your part.

THE CLERGYMAN. Then on what ground? Oh, I shouldnt have kissed her.

MRS HYERING. Oho! You said it was she who kissed you.

THE CLERGYMAN. Yes: I know I should have explained that. But she let me kiss her.

MRS HYERING. That must have been a thrill, Mr Hammingtap.

Life came to you that time, didnt it?

THE CLERGYMAN. Oh please, I cant speak of it. But why should she reject me if I make her an honorable proposal?

LADY FARWATERS. Because she will consider your honorable proposal dishonorable, Mr Hammingtap, unless it includes all the ladies of the family. You will not be allowed to pick and choose and make distinctions. You marry all or none.

THE CLERGYMAN. Oh dear! My poor little brain is giving way. I cant make sense of what you are saying. I know that your meaning must be perfectly right and respectable, Lady Farwaters; but it sounds like a dreadful sort of wickedness.

LADY FARWATERS. May I try to explain?

THE CLERGYMAN. Please do, Lady Farwaters. But I wish you wouldnt call me Mr Hammingtap. I am accustomed to be called Iddy among friends.

MRS HYERING. What does Iddy stand for?

THE CLERGYMAN. Well, in our home I was known as the idiot.

MRS HYERING. Oh! I am sorry: I didnt know.

THE CLERGYMAN. Not at all. My sister was the Kiddy; so I became the Iddy. Do please call me that. And be kind to me. I am weakminded and lose my head very easily; and I can see that you are all wonderfully clever and strongminded. That is why I could be so happy here. I can take in anything if you will only tell it to me in a gentle hushabyebaby sort of way and call me Iddy. Now go on, Lady Farwaters. Excuse me for interrupting you so long.

LADY FARWATERS. You see, Iddy—

IDDY. Oh, thanks!

LADY FARWATERS [continuing] —our four children are not like European children and not like Asiatic children. They have the east in their brains and the west in their blood. And at the same time they have the east in their blood and the west in their brains. Well, from the time when as tiny tots they could speak, they invented fairy stories. I thought it silly and dangerous, and wanted to stop them; but Prola would not let me: she taught them a game called the heavenly parliament in which all of them told tales and added them to the general stock until a fairyland was built up, with laws and religious rituals, and finally a great institution which they called the Superfamily. It began by my telling them in my old conventional English way to love oneanother; but they would not have that at all: they said it was vulgar nonsense and made them interfere with oneanother and hate oneanother. Then they hit out for themselves the idea that they were not to love oneanother, but that they were to be oneanother.

IDDY. To be oneanother! I dont understand.

SIR CHARLES. Neither do I. Pra and Prola think they understand it; but Lady Farwaters and I dont; and we dont pretend to. We are too English. But the practical side of it—the side that concerns you—is that Vashti and Maya are now grown up. They must have children. The boys will need a young wife.

IDDY. You mean two wives.

LADY FARWATERS. Oh, a dozen, if so many of the right sort can be found.

IDDY. But—but—but that would be polygamy.

PROLA. You are in the east, Mr Iddy. The east is polygamous. Try to remember that polygamists form an enormous majority of the subjects of the British Empire, and that you are not now in Clapham.

IDDY. How dreadful! I never thought of that.

LADY FARWATERS. And the girls will need a young husband.

IDDY [imploringly] Two young husbands, Lady Farwaters. Oh please, two.

LADY FARWATERS. I think not, at first.

IDDY. Oh! But I am not an oriental. I am a clergyman of the Church of England.

HYERING. That means nothing to Vashti.

PRA. And still less to Maya.

IDDY. But—but—oh dear! dont you understand? I want to marry Maya. And if I marry Maya I cannot marry Vashti. An English clergyman could not marry two women.

LADY FARWATERS. From their point of view they are not two women: they are one. Vashti is Maya; and Maya is Vashti.

47

IDDY. But even if such a thing were possible how could I be faithful to Vashti without being unfaithful to Maya? I couldnt bear to be unfaithful to Maya.

LADY FARWATERS. Maya would regard the slightest unfaithfulness to Vashti as a betrayal of herself and a breach of your marriage vow.

IDDY. But thats nonsense: utter nonsense. Please dont put such things into my head. I am trying so hard to keep sane; but you are terrifying me. If only I could bring myself never to see Maya again I should rush out of this garden and make for home. But it would be like rushing out of heaven. I am most unhappy; and yet I am dreadfully happy. I think I am under some sort of enchantment.

MRS HYERING. Well, stick to the enchantment while it lasts. Let life come to you.

PRA. May I remind you that not only Vashti and Maya, but all the ladies here, are included in the superfamily compact.

IDDY. Oh, how nice and comfortable that would be! They would be mothers to me.

PROLA [rebuking Pra] Let him alone, Pra. There is such a thing as calf love. Vashti and Maya are quite enough for him to begin with. Maya has already driven him half mad. There is no need for us old people to drive him quite out of his senses. [She rises] This has gone far enough. Wait here alone, Mr Hammingtap, to collect your thoughts. Look at the flowers; breathe the air; open your soul to the infinite space of the sky. Nature always helps.

IDDY [rising] Thank you, Lady Prola. Yes: that will be a great help.

PROLA. Come. [She goes up the steps and into the house].

They all rise and follow her, each bestowing a word of counsel or comfort on the distracted clergyman.

PRA. Relax. Take a full breath and then relax. Do not strangle yourself with useless anxieties. [He goes].

LADY FARWATERS. Cast out fear, Iddy. Warm heart. Clear mind. Think of having a thousand friends, a thousand wives, a thousand mothers. [She pats him on the shoulder and goes].

48

SIR CHARLES. Stand up to it, my boy. The world is changing. Stand up to it. [*He goes*].

MRS HYERING. Dont let that conscience of yours worry you. Let life come to you. [*She goes*].

HYERING. Try to sleep a little. The morning has been too much for you. [*He goes*].

IDDY. Sleep! I will not sleep. They want me to disgrace my cloth; but I wont. I wont relax: I wont disobey my conscience: I wont smell those flowers: I wont look at the sky. Nature is not good for me here. Nature is eastern here: it's poison to an Englishman. I will think of England and tighten myself up and pull myself together. England! The Malverns! the Severn plain! the Welsh border! the three cathedrals! England that is me: I that am England! Damn and blast all these tropical paradises: I am an English clergyman; and my place is in England. Floreat Etona! Back to England and all that England means to an Englishman! In this sign I shall conquer. [*He turns resolutely to go out as he came in, and finds himself face to face with Maya, who has stolen in and listened gravely and intently to his exhortation.*

IDDY [*collapsing in despair on the parapet of the well*] Oh, Maya, let me go, let me go.

MAYA [*sinking beside him with her arm round his neck*] Speak to me from your soul, and not with words that you have picked up in the street.

IDDY. Respect my cloth, Miss Farwaters.

MAYA. Maya. Maya is my name. I am the veil of the temple. Rend me in twain.

IDDY. I wont. I will go home and marry some honest English girl named Polly Perkins. [*Shuddering in her embrace*] Oh, Maya, darling: speak to me like a human being.

MAYA. That is how I speak to you; but you do not recognize human speech when you hear it: you crave for slang and small talk, and for readymade phrases that mean nothing. Speak from your soul; and tell me: do you love Vashti? Would you die for Vashti?

IDDY. No.

MAYA [*with a flash of rage, springing up*] Wretch! [*Calmly and conclusively*] You are free. Farewell [*She points his way through the house*].

IDDY [*clutching at her robe*] No, no. Do not leave me. I love you—you. I would die for you. That sounds like a word picked up in the street; but it is true. I would die for you ten times over.

MAYA. It is not true. Words, words, words out of the gutter. Vashti and Maya are one: you cannot love me if you do not love Vashti: you cannot die for me without dying for Vashti.

IDDY. Oh, I assure you I can.

MAYA. Lies, lies. If you can feel one heart throb for me that is not a throb for Vashti: if for even an instant there are two women in your thoughts instead of one, then you do not know what love can be.

IDDY. But it's just the contrary. I—

VASHTI [*who has entered silently, sits beside him and throws an arm round his shoulders*] Do you not love me? Would you not die for me?

IDDY. [*mesmerized by her eyes*] Oh DEAR!!! Yes: your eyes make my heart melt: your voice opens heaven to me: I love you. I would die a thousand times for you.

VASHTI. And Maya? You love Maya. You would die a million times for Maya?

IDDY. Yes, yes. I would die for either, for both: for one, for the other—

MAYA. For Vashti Maya?

IDDY. For Vashti Maya, for Maya Vashti.

VASHTI. Your lives and ours are one life.

MAYA [*sitting down beside him*] And this is the Kingdom of love.

The three embrace with interlaced arms and vanish in black darkness.

ACT II

A fine forenoon some years later. The garden is unchanged; but inside the distant breakwater the harbor is crowded with cruisers; and on the lawn near the steps is a writing table littered with papers and furnished with a wireless telephone. Sir Charles is sitting at the end of it with his back to the house. Seated near him is Pra. Both are busy writing. Hyering enters.

SIR CHARLES. Morning, Hyering.

HYERING. Morning. [*He sits at the other end of the table after waving an acknowledgment of Pra's indication of a salaam*]. Anything fresh?

SIR CHARLES [*pointing to the roadstead*] Look! Five more cruisers in last night. The papers say it is the first time the fleets of the British Empire have ever assembled in one place.

HYERING. I hope it will never happen again. If we dont get rid of them quickly there will be the biggest naval battle on record. They are quarrelling already like Kilkenny cats.

SIR CHARLES. What about?

HYERING. Oh, about everything. About moorings, about firing salutes: which has the right to fire first? about flags, about shore parties, about nothing. We shall never be able to keep the peace between them. The Quebec has got alongside the Belfast. The Quebec has announced Mass at eleven on All Saints Day; and the Belfast has announced firing practice at the same hour. Do you see that sloop that came in last night?

SIR CHARLES. What is it?

HYERING. The Pitcairn Island fleet. They are Seventh Day Adventists, and are quite sure the Judgment Day is fixed for five o'clock this afternoon. They propose to do nothing until then but sing hymns. The Irish Free State admiral threatens to sink them if they dont stop. How am I to keep them quiet?

PRA. Dont keep them quiet. Their squabbles will make them forget what they were sent here for.

HYERING. Forget! not they. I have six ultimatums from their admirals, all expiring at noon today. Look. [*He takes a batch of letters from his pocket and throws them on the table*].

SIR CHARLES [*pointing to the letters on the table*] Look at these!

PRA. All about Iddy.

SIR CHARLES. Iddy has got into the headlines at home. The cables are humming with Iddy. Iddy has convulsed the Empire, confound him!

HYERING. Anything fresh from London or Delhi?

SIR CHARLES. The same old songs. The Church of England wont tolerate polygamy on any terms, and insists on our prosecuting Iddy if we cannot whitewash him. Delhi declares that any attempt to persecute polygamy would be an insult to the religions of India.

PRA. The Cultural Minister at Delhi adds a postscript to say that as he has been married two hundred and thirtyfour times, and could not have lived on his salary without the dowries, the protest of the Church of England shews a great want of consideration for his position. He has a hundred and seventeen children surviving.

SIR CHARLES. Then there's a chap I never heard of, calling himself the Caliph of British Islam. He demands that Iddy shall put away all his wives except four.

HYERING. What does the Foreign Office say to that?

PRA. The Foreign Office hails it as a happy solution of a difficulty that threatened to be very serious.

HYERING. What do you think about it all yourself, Pra?

PRA. Think! Thought has no place in such discussions. Each of them must learn that its ideas are not everybody's ideas. Here is a cablegram from the League of British Imperial Womanhood, Vancouver and Pretoria. "Burn him alive and his hussies with him." Do you expect me to think about such people?

HYERING. Nobody has made any practical suggestion, I suppose?

PRA. The United States intervene with a friendly suggestion that the parties should be divorced. But the Irish Free State will

not hear of divorce, and points out that if the parties become
Catholics their marriages can be annulled with the greatest ease.

HYERING. Oh, the west! the west! the west!

PRA. Oh, the east! the east! the east! I tried to reconcile them;
and I had only two successes: you and Lady Farwaters.

HYERING. You kicked me into the sea.

SIR CHARLES. You made love to Lady Farwaters.

PRA. I had to use that method with very crude novices; and
Lady Farwaters, with her English ladylike bringing-up, was so
crude that she really could not understand any purely intellectual
appeal. Your own mind, thanks to your public school and university, was in an even worse condition; and Prola had to convert
you by the same elementary method. Well, it has worked, up to
a point. The insight you obtained into eastern modes of thought
has enabled you to govern the eastern crown colonies with extraordinary success. Downing Street hated you; but Delhi sup-
ported you; and since India won Dominion status Delhi has been
the centre of the British Empire. You, Hyering, have had the
same diplomatic success in the east for the same reason. But beyond this we have been unable to advance a step. Our dream of
founding a millennial world culture: the dream which united
Prola and Pra as you first knew them, and then united us all six,
has ended in a single little household with four children, wonderful and beautiful, but sterile. When we had to find a husband for
the blossoming girls, only one man was found capable of merging
himself in the unity of the family: a man fed on air from his childhood. And how has this paragon turned out? An impotent simpleton. It would be impossible to conceive a human being of less
consequence in the world. And yet, look! There is the Imperial
Armada, in which every petty province insists on its separate fleet,
every trumpery islet its battleship, its cruiser, or at least its sloop
or gunboat! Why are they here, armed to the teeth, threatening
what they call their sanctions? a word that once meant the ap-
proval of the gods, and now means bombs full of poison gas.
Solely on account of the simpleton. To reform his morals, half of
them want to rain destruction on this little household of ours, and

the other half is determined to sink them if they attempt it.

HYERING. They darent use their bombs, you know.

PRA. True; but what is to prevent them from taking to their fists and coming ashore to fight it out on the beach with sticks and bottles and stones, or with their fists? What do the ultimatums say, Hyering?

HYERING [*reading them*] Number one from the English admiral. "If the polygamist-adulterer Hammingtap is not handed over by noon tomorrow" that is today "I shall be obliged to open fire on Government House." Number two, from the commander of the Bombay Squadron. "Unless an unequivocal guarantee of the safety and liberty of Mr Hammingtap be in my hands by noon to-day" that came this morning "I shall land a shore party equipped with machine guns and tear gas bombs to assist the local police in the protection of his person." Number three: "I have repeatedly informed you that the imperial province of Holy Island demands the immediate and exemplary combustion of the abominable libertine and damnable apostate known as Phosfor Hammingtap. The patience of the Holy Island fleet will be exhausted at noon on the 13th" today "and the capital of the Unexpected Islands must take the consequences." Number four—

SIR CHARLES. Oh, bother number four! They are all the same: not one of them has originality enough to fix half-past-eleven or a quarter-to-one.

HYERING. By the way, Pra, have you taken any steps? I havnt.

PRA. Yes I have. Dont worry. I have sent a message.

SIR CHARLES. What message?

PRA. The Mayor of the Port earnestly begs the commanders of the imperial fleet to suspend action for another day, as his attention is urgently occupied by a serious outbreak of smallpox in the harbor district.

SIR CHARLES. Good. [*The boom of a cannon interrupts him*] There goes the noonday cannon!

HYERING. I hope they got the message in time.

The garden and its occupants vanish. When they reappear, the harbor is empty: not a ship is visible. The writing table, with its chairs and papers, has been removed and replaced by a small tea-table. Tea is ready. The wireless telephone is still there.

Vashti and Maya are in their shrines. Lady Farwaters is sitting on the western stone seat, with Mrs Hyering beside her on her right. Prola is sitting on the eastern seat. All five ladies are taking tea.

Pra comes from the house with Sir Charles and Hyering. They help themselves to tea. Pra abstains.

SIR CHARLES. Not a blessed ship left in the harbor! Your message certainly did the trick, Pra. [*He sits down beside Prola, on her left*].

PRA [*sitting down between the two British ladies*] They may come back.

HYERING [*sitting beside Prola, on her right*] Not a bit of it. By the time the fleet realizes that it has been humbugged the Empire will be tired of Iddy.

VASHTI. The world is tired of Iddy.

MAYA. *I* am tired of Iddy.

VASHTI. Iddy is a pestilence.

MAYA. Iddy is a bore.

VASHTI. Let us throw ourselves into the sea to escape from Iddy.

MAYA. Let us throw Iddy into the sea that he may escape from himself.

VASHTI. You are wise, Prola. Tell us how to get rid of Iddy.

MAYA. We cannot endure Iddy for ever, Prola.

PROLA. You two chose him, not I.

MAYA. We were young: we did not know.

VASHTI. Help us, Pra. You have lost faith in us; but your wits are still keen.

MAYA. Pra: we beseech thee. Abolish the incubus.

VASHTI. Give him peace that we may have rest.

MAYA. Give him rest that we may have peace.

VASHTI. Let him be as he was before we knew him.

MAYA. When we were happy.

VASHTI. When he was innocent.

PRA. You raised this strange spirit. I cannot exorcise him.

VASHTI. Rather than endure him I will empty the heavens of their rain and dew.

MAYA. Silence him, O ye stars.

Iddy comes from the house in a condition of lazy self-complacence. He is received in dead silence. Nobody looks at him. He pours himself out a cup of tea. The silence becomes grim. He sits down on the grass at Prola's feet, and sips his tea. The silence continues.

IDDY [*at last*] I am a futile creature.

They all turn as if stung and look at him. Then they resume their attitudes of deadly endurance.

IDDY. It is a terrible thing to be loved. I dont suppose any man has ever been loved as I have been loved, or loved as I have loved. But there's not so much in it as people say. I am writing a sermon about it. It is a sermon on Eternity.

They look at him as before.

IDDY. The line I am going to take is this. We have never been able to imagine eternity properly. St John of Patmos started the notion of playing harps and singing praises for ever and ever. But the organist tells me that composers have to use the harp very sparingly because, though it makes a very pretty effect at first, you get tired of it so soon. You couldnt go on playing the harp for ever; and if you sang "Worthy is the Lamb" for ever you would drive the Lamb mad. The notion is that you cant have too much of a good thing; but you can: you can bear hardship much longer than you could bear heaven. Love is like music. Music is very nice: the organist says that when the wickedness of mankind tempts him to despair he comforts himself by remembering that the human race produced Mozart; but a woman who plays the piano all day is a curse. A woman who makes love to you all day is much worse; and yet nothing is lovelier than love, up to a point. We all love one another here in a wonderful way: I love Vashti, I love Maya, I love Prola; and they all love me so wonderfully that their three loves are only one love. But it is my belief that some day we'll have to try something else. If we dont we'll come to hate one another.

VASHTI. If it is any consolation to you, Iddy, I can assure you that I already hate you so intensely that if it were in my nature to kill anything I should kill you.

IDDY. There now! I ought to be wounded and horrified; but I'm not: I feel as if youd given me a strawberry ice. Thank you, dear Vashti, thank you. You give me hope that even Maya will get tired of me someday.

MAYA. I have been on the point of beating you to a jelly for ever so long past; but just as my fists were clenched to do it you always managed to come out with some stroke of idiocy that was either so funny or so piteous that I have kissed you instead.

IDDY. You make me happier than I have been for months. But, you know, that does not settle my difficulties. I dont know whether other people are like me or not—

LADY FARWATERS. No, Iddy: you are unique.

IDDY. Anyhow, I have made a discovery as regards myself.

VASHTI. Enough is known already.

MAYA. Seek no further: there is nothing there.

VASHTI. There never has been anything.

IDDY. Shut up, you two. This is something really interesting. I am writing a second sermon.

ALL THE REST [gasp] !!!!!!!

PRA. Was eternity not long enough for one sermon?

IDDY. This one is on love.

VASHTI [springing up] I will cast myself down from a precipice.

MAYA [springing up] I will gas myself.

IDDY. Oh, not until you have heard my sermon, please.

PROLA. Listen to him, children. Respect the wisdom of the fool.

VASHTI [resuming her goddess-in-a-shrine attitude] The oracles of the wise are unheeded. Silence for the King of Idiots.

MAYA [also enshrining herself] Speak, Solomon.

IDDY. Well, the discovery I have made is that we were commanded to love our enemies because loving is good for us and dreadfully bad for them. I love you all here intensely; and I enjoy loving you. I love Vashti; I love Maya; and I adore Prola with a passion that grows and deepens from year to year.

PROLA. Dolt! I am too old.

IDDY. You were never young and you will never be old. You are the way and the light for me. But you have never loved me and never will love me. You have never loved anything human: why should you? Nothing human is good enough to be loved. But every decent human creature has some capacity for loving. Look at me! What a little worm I am! My sermons are wretched stuff, except these last two, which I think really have something in them. I cannot bear being loved, because I know that I am a worm, and that nobody could love me unless they were completely deluded as to my merits. But I can love, and delight in loving. I love Vashti for hating me, because she is quite right to hate me: her hatred is a proof of her beautiful clear judgment. I love Maya for being out of all patience with me, because I know that I am enough to drive anybody mad, and she is wise enough to know how worthless I am. I love Prola because she is far above loving or hating me; and there is something about her dark beauty that—

PROLA [kicking him] Silence, simpleton. Let the unspeakable remain unspoken.

IDDY. I dont mind your kicking me, Prola: you understand; and that is enough for me. And now you see what a jolly fine sermon it will be, and why I shall be so happy here with you from this day on. For I have the joy of loving you all without the burden of being loved in return, or the falsehood of being idolized.

MAYA. Solomon has spoken.

VASHTI. Stupendous.

LADY FARWATERS. Do not mock, darlings. There is something in what he says.

MAYA [desperately] But how are we to get rid of him? He is settling down with us for life.

VASHTI. We have brought him on ourselves.

MAYA. We cannot make him hate us.

VASHTI. He will go with us to heaven.

MAYA. In the depths of hell he will find us.

Kanchin and Janga enter processionally, reading newspapers.

KANCHIN. News!

JANGA. News!

They sit enshrined, foursquare with their sisters.

KANCHIN. By wireless.

JANGA. Tomorrow's three o'clock edition.

KANCHIN. The land that brought forth Iddy begins the Apocalypse.

HYERING. What do you mean? Has anything happened in England?

KANCHIN. England has broken loose.

SIR CHARLES. What do you mean? broken loose. Read the news, man. Out with it.

KANCHIN [*reading the headlines*] Dissolution of the British Empire.

JANGA [*reading*] Withdrawal of England from the Empire.

KANCHIN. England strikes for independence.

JANGA. Downing Street declares for a right little tight little island.

KANCHIN. The British Prime Minister cuts the cable and gives the new slogan.

JANGA. Back to Elizabeth's England; and to hell with the empire!

KANCHIN. Ireland to the rescue!

JANGA. Free State President declares Ireland cannot permit England to break the unity of the Empire. Ireland will lead the attack on treason and disruption.

KANCHIN. The Prime Minister's reply to the President suppressed as unprintable.

JANGA. Canada claims position of premier Dominion left vacant by the secession of England.

KANCHIN. Australia counterclaims as metropolitan dominion.

JANGA. New Zealand proclaims a butter blockade until its claim to precedence is recognized by Australia.

KANCHIN. South Africa renames Capetown Empire City, and gives notice to all Britishers to clear out of Africa within ten days.

JANGA. His Holiness the Pope calls on all Christendom to celebrate the passing away of the last vain dream of earthly empire, and the unity of all living souls in the Catholic Kingdom of God and his Church.

LADY FARWATERS. That sounds like the voice of a grown-up man through the whooping of a pack of schoolboys.

JANGA [*prosaically*] So far, there have been no disturbances and little popular interest.

KANCHIN. The various international Boards are carrying on as usual.

JANGA. Today's football—

PROLA. No, Janga: certainly not.

SIR CHARLES. But what becomes of our jobs as Governor and political secretary, Hyering? Will this affect our salaries?

HYERING. They will stop: that is all. We had better proclaim the Unexpected Isles an independent republic and secure the new jobs for ourselves.

VASHTI. The world is tired of republics and their jobberies. Proclaim a kingdom.

MAYA. Or a queendom.

IDDY. Oh yes: let us make Prola queen. And I shall be her chaplain.

PRA. By all means, as far as I am concerned. Prola has always been the real ruler here.

VASHTI. Prola is she who decides.

MAYA. Prola is she who unites.

VASHTI. Prola is she who knows.

MAYA. No one can withstand Prola.

PROLA. Be quiet, you two. You shall not make an idol of me.

KANCHIN. We shall make you Empress of the Isles.

JANGA. Prola the First.

VASHTI. Homage, Prola.

MAYA. Love, Prola.

KANCHIN. Obedience, Prola.

JANGA. Absolute rule, Prola.

PROLA. All your burdens on me. Lazy idle children.

KANCHIN. Hurrah! All burdens on Prola.

JANGA. The burden of thought.

VASHTI. The burden of knowledge.

MAYA. The burden of righteousness.

VASHTI. The burden of justice.

MAYA. The burden of mercy.

PROLA. Cease, cease: these are not burdens to me: they are the air I breathe. I shall rule you as I have always done because you are too lazy to rule yourselves.

HYERING. You can rule us, Prola. But will the public ever understand you?

PRA. They will obey her. They would not do that if they understood.

IDDY. I have just been thinking—

MAYA. Solomon has been thinking.

VASHTI. Thoughts without brains.

IDDY. Will the Antiphonal Quartet, if it wants to give another concert, kindly remove itself out of hearing.

KANCHIN. Silence for the Prophet.

JANGA. Mum!

VASHTI. Dumb.

MAYA. Tiddy iddy um. Carry on, darling.

IDDY. Prola can rule this house because she knows what is happening in it. But how is she to be an Empress if she doesnt know what is happening everywhere?

MRS HYERING. She can read the newspapers, cant she, silly?

IDDY. Yes; but fifteen years later, when the statesmen write their memoirs and autobiographies and publish them, we shall find that it never happened at all and what really happened was quite different. We dont know the truth about any of our statesmen until they are dead and cant take libel actions. Nobody knows the sort of people we really are. The papers have been full of us for weeks past; and not a single word they say about us is true. They think I am a sort of Mahdi or Mad Mullah, and that Prola and Vashti and Maya are a troop of immoral dancing girls, and that Sir Charles is a voluptuous sultan and Hyering a co-respond-ent. They dont live in a world of truth: they live in a world of their own ideas, which have nothing to do with our ideas. Consequently—Therefore—er—er— What was I going to say, Pra? My brain is not strong enough to keep the thread of my remarks. I ought to have written it down.

PRA. What you have arrived at is that we cannot live in a world of political facts, because we shall not know the political facts for years to come. We must therefore live in a world of original ideas, created by ourselves out of our own nature.

IDDY. Yes. We mustnt pretend to be omniscient. Even God would not be omniscient if He read the newspapers. We must have an ideal of a beautiful and good world. We must believe that to establish that beautiful and good world on earth is the best thing we can do, and the only sort of religion and politics that is worth bothering about.

PROLA. What about the people who have no original ideas, Iddy?

PRA. The great majority of mankind?

IDDY. Theyll be only too glad to do what you tell them, Prola, if you can make them feel that it's right.

PROLA. And if they are incapable of feeling it?

JANGA. Kill.

KANCHIN. Kill.

VASHTI. Kill.

MAYA. Kill.

PROLA. They can do that as easily as I. Any fool can. And there are more of them.

JANGA. Set them to kill one another; and rule.

KANCHIN. Divide and govern.

VASHTI. Feed them on splendid words.

MAYA. Dazzle them with our beauty.

MRS HYERING. Well I never!

IDDY [rising] Excuse me. I'm going into the house to get the field glass. [He goes up the steps].

MRS HYERING. Whatever do you want the field glass for?

IDDY [*pointing to the sky*] There's a strange bird flying about there. I think it's an albatross. [*He goes into the house*].

VASHTI, MAYA, KANCHIN, JANGA [*hissing after him*] Liar. Baby. Dastard. Hypocrite.

SIR CHARLES [*laughing*] An albatross! Now would anybody in the world, over the age of six, except Iddy, invent such a ridiculous excuse for going to his room to indulge in his poor little secret vice of cigaret smoking?

MAYA. Faugh! The unkissable.

VASHTI. The air poisoner.

KANCHIN. The albatrocity.

MAYA. VASHTI. JANGA [*shocked by the pun*] Oh!!

LADY FARWATERS. Cant you four darlings do something useful instead of sitting there deafening us with your slogans?

KANCHIN [*springing erect*] Yes, action. Action!

JANGA [*rising similarly*] No more of this endless talk! talk! talk!

VASHTI. Yes, action! daring! Let us rob.

MAYA. Let us shoot.

KANCHIN. Let us die for something.

JANGA. For our flag and for our Empress.

VASHTI. For our country, right or wrong.

MAYA. Let there be sex appeal. Let the women make the men brave.

KANCHIN. We must defend our homes.

JANGA. Our women.

VASHTI. Our native soil.

MAYA. It is sweet to die for one's country.

VASHTI. It is glorious to outface death.

ALL FOUR. Yes. Death! death! Glory! glory!

PROLA. Hold your tongues, you young whelps. Is this what we have brought you up for?

PRA. Stop screaming about nothing, will you. Use your minds.

MAYA. We have no minds.

VASHTI. We have imaginations.

KANCHIN. We have made this house a temple.

JANGA. We have made Prola its goddess.

MAYA. We have made it a palace.

VASHTI. A palace for Queen Prola.

KANCHIN. She shall reign.

JANGA. For ever and ever.

VASHTI AND MAYA [*in unison*] Hail, Prola, our goddess!

KANCHIN AND JANGA [*in unison*] Hail, Prola, our empress!

ALL FOUR [*rushing down to the lawn and throwing themselves on their knees before her*] Hail!

PROLA. Will you provoke me to box your ears, you abominable idolaters. Get up this instant. Go and scrub the floors. Do anything that is dirty and grubby and smelly enough to shew that you live in a real world and not in a fool's paradise. If I catch you grovelling to me, a creature of the same clay as yourselves, but fortunately for you with a little more common sense, I will beat the slavishness out of your bones.

MAYA. Oh, what ecstasy to be beaten by Prola!

VASHTI. To feel her rule in the last extremity of pain!

KANCHIN. To suffer for her!

JANGA. To die for her!

PROLA. Get out, all four. My empire is not of such as you. Begone.

MAYA. How lovely is obedience! [*She makes an obeisance and runs away through the garden*].

VASHTI. Obedience is freedom from the intolerable fatigue of thought. [*She makes her obeisance and sails away, disappearing between the garden and the house*].

KANCHIN. You speak as an empress should speak. [*He salaams and bounds off after Maya*].

JANGA. The voice of authority gives us strength and unity. Command us always thus: it is what we need and love. [*He strides away in Vashti's footsteps*].

PROLA. An excuse for leaving everything to me. Lazy, lazy, lazy! Someday Heaven will get tired of lazy people; and the Pitcairn Islanders will see their Day of Judgment at last.

A distant fusillade of shotguns answers her.

SIR CHARLES. Shooting! What can the matter be?

They all rise and listen anxiously.

A trumpet call rings out from the sky.

HYERING. Where on earth did that come from? There is not such a thing as a trumpet in the island.

The four come rushing back into the garden, wildly excited.

KANCHIN. Look, look, quick! The albatross.

PRA [*rising*] The albatross!!

MAYA. Yes: Iddy's albatross. Look!

JANGA. Flying all over the town.

VASHTI [*pointing*] There it goes. See.

A second fusillade of shotguns, much nearer.

MAYA. Oh, theyre all trying to shoot it. Brutes!

KANCHIN. They havnt hit it. Here it comes.

MAYA. It's flying this way.

VASHTI. It's swooping down.

Iddy comes from the house and trots down the steps with a field glass in his hand.

IDDY. Ive been looking at it through the window for the last five minutes. It isnt an albatross. Look at it through this. [*He hands the glass to Pra*].

KANCHIN. Then what is it?

IDDY. I think it's an angel.

JANGA. Oh get out, you silly idiot.

PRA [*looking through the glass*] That is no bird.

An angel flies down into the middle of the garden. General stupefaction. He shakes himself. Quantities of bullets and small shot fall from his wings and clothes.

THE ANGEL. Really, your people ought to know better than to shoot at an angel.

MAYA. Are you an angel?

THE ANGEL. Well, what do you suppose I am?

F

VASHTI. Of course he is an angel. Look at his wings.

THE ANGEL. Attention, please! Have you not heard the trumpet? This is the Judgment Day.

ALL THE REST. The what???!!!

THE ANGEL. The Judgment Day. The Day of Judgment.

SIR CHARLES. Well I'll be damned!

THE ANGEL. Very possibly.

HYERING. Do you mean that the Pitcairn Islanders were right after all?!

THE ANGEL. Yes. You are all now under judgment, in common with the rest of the English speaking peoples. Dont gape at me as if you had never seen an angel before.

PROLA. But we never have.

THE ANGEL [*relaxing*] True. Ha ha ha! Well, you thoroughly understand, dont you, that your records are now being looked into with a view to deciding whether you are worth your salt or not.

PRA. And suppose it is decided that we are not worth our salt?

THE ANGEL [*reassuring them in a pleasantly offhanded manner*] Then you will simply disappear: that is all. You will no longer exist. Dont let me keep you all standing. Sit down if you like. Never mind me: sitting and standing are all alike to an angel. However— [*he sits down on the parapet of the well*].

They sit as before, the four superchildren enshrining themselves as usual.

The telephone rings. Hyering rises and takes it.

HYERING [*to the angel*] Excuse me. [*To the telephone*] Yes? Hyering speaking. . . . Somebody what? . . . . Oh! somebody fooling on the wireless. Well, theyre not fooling: an angel has just landed here to tell us the same thing. . . . An angel. A for arrowroot, N for nitrogen, G for— thats it: an angel. . . . Well, after all, the Judgment Day had to come some day, hadnt it? Why not this day as well as another? . . . . I'll ask the angel about it and ring you later. Goodbye. [*He rings off*]. Look here, angel. The wireless has been on all over Europe. London reports the Judgment Day in full swing; but Paris knows nothing about it; Hilversum knows

nothing about it; Berlin, Rome, Madrid, and Geneva know nothing about it; and Moscow says the British bourgeoisie has been
driven mad by its superstitions. How do you account for that? If
it is the Judgment Day in England it must be the Judgment Day
everywhere.

THE ANGEL. Why?

HYERING [*sitting down*] Well, it stands to reason.

THE ANGEL. Does it? Would it be reasonable to try cases in hundreds of different lands and languages and creeds and colors on
the same day in the same place? Of course not. The whole business will last longer than what you call a year. We gave the English
speaking folk the first turn in compliment to one of your big guns
—a dean—name of Inge, I think. I announced it to him last night
in a dream, and asked him whether the English would appreciate
the compliment. He said he thought they would prefer to put it
off as long as possible, but that they needed it badly and he was
ready. The other languages will follow. The United States of
America will be tried tomorrow, Australasia next day, Scotland
next, then Ireland—

LADY FARWATERS. But excuse me: they do not speak different
languages.

THE ANGEL. They sound different to us.

SIR CHARLES. I wonder how they are taking it in England.

THE ANGEL. I am afraid most of them are incapable of understanding the ways of heaven. They go motoring or golfing on
Sundays instead of going to church; and they never open a Bible.
When you mention Adam and Eve, or Cain and Abel, to say nothing of the Day of Judgment, they dont know what you are talking
about. The others—the pious ones—think we have come to dig
up all the skeletons and put them through one of their shocking
criminal trials. They actually expect us to make angels of them
for ever and ever.

MRS HYERING. See here, angel. This isnt a proper sort of Judgment Day. It's a fine day. It's like Bank Holiday.

THE ANGEL. And pray why should the Day of Judgment not
be a fine day?

MRS HYERING. Well, it's hardly what we were led to expect, you know.

JANGA. "The heavens shall pass away with a great noise."

KANCHIN. "The elements shall melt with fervent heat."

JANGA. "The earth also and the works that are therein shall be burnt up."

VASHTI. The stars are fixed in their courses. They have not fallen to the earth.

MAYA. The heavens are silent. Where are the seven thunders?

VASHTI. The seven vials full of the wrath of God?

JANGA. The four horses?

KANCHIN. The two witnesses?

THE ANGEL. My good people, if you want these things you must provide them for yourselves. If you want a great noise, you have your cannons. If you want a fervent heat to burn up the earth you have your high explosives. If you want vials of wrath to rain down on you, they are ready in your arsenals, full of poison gases. Some years ago you had them all in full play, burning up the earth and spreading death, famine, and pestilence. But the spring came and created life faster than you could destroy it. The birds sang over your trenches; and their promise of summer was fulfilled. The sun that shone undisturbed on your pitiful Day of Wrath shines today over Heaven's Day of Judgment. It will continue to light us and warm us; and there will be no noise nor wrath nor fire nor thunder nor destruction nor plagues nor terrors of any sort. I am afraid you will find it very dull.

LADY FARWATERS [*politely*] Not at all. Pray dont think that.

MRS HYERING. Well, a little good manners never does any harm; but I tell you straight, Mister Angel, I cant feel as if there was anything particular happening, in spite of you and your wings. Ive only just had my tea; and I cant feel a bit serious without any preparation or even an organ playing.

THE ANGEL. You will feel serious enough presently when things begin to happen.

MRS HYERING. Yes; but what things?

THE ANGEL. What was foretold to you. "His angels shall gather

together his elect. Then shall two be in the field: the one shall be
taken and the other left. Two women shall be grinding at the mill.
The one shall be taken and the other left."

MRS HYERING. But which? Thats what I want to know.

PROLA. There is nothing new in this taking of the one and leaving the other: natural death has always been doing it.

THE ANGEL. Natural death does it senselessly, like a blind child
throwing stones. We angels are executing a judgment. The lives
which have no use, no meaning, no purpose, will fade out. You
will have to justify your existence or perish. Only the elect shall
survive.

MRS HYERING. But where does the end of the world come in?

THE ANGEL. The Day of Judgment is not the end of the world,
but the end of its childhood and the beginning of its responsible
maturity. So now you know; and my business with you is ended.
[*He rises*]. Is there any way of getting out on the roof of this
house?

SIR CHARLES [*rising*] Certainly: it is a flat roof where we often
sit. [*He leads the way to the house*].

KANCHIN. In theory.

JANGA. In fact we never sit there.

THE ANGEL. That does not matter. All I want is a parapet to
take off from. Like the albatross, I cannot rise from the ground
without great difficulty. An angel is far from being the perfect
organism you imagine. There is always something better.

VASHTI. Excelsior.

ALL FOUR [*rising and singing vociferously*] Eck-cel-see-orr! Eck-
cel-see-or!

THE ANGEL [*putting his fingers in his ears*] Please, no. In heaven
we are tired of singing. It is not done now. [*He follows Sir Charles
out*].

KANCHIN. Lets see him take off.

*The four rush up the garden and look up at the roof. The others
rise and watch.*

JANGA [*calling up*] Start into the wind, old man. Spring off
hard, from the ball of the foot. Dont fall on us.

KANCHIN. Oopsh! Off he goes.

The beating of the angel's wings is heard.

VASHTI. He makes a noise like a vacuum cleaner.

MAYA [*wafting kisses*] Goodbye, silly old Excelsior.

The noise stops.

JANGA. His wings have stopped beating. He is soaring up the wind.

KANCHIN. He is getting smaller and smaller. His speed must be terrific.

MAYA. He is too small for an albatross.

VASHTI. He is smaller than a canary.

KANCHIN. He is out of sight.

MAYA. There! One last glint of the sun on his wings. He is gone.

The four troop back and resume their seats. The others sit as before, except that Iddy deserts Prola and sits on the well parapet. Sir Charles returns from the house with a batch of wireless messages in his hand.

SIR CHARLES [*sitting in his former place*] Well, my dears: the Judgment Day is over, it seems.

IDDY. I cant believe it was really the Judgment Day.

PRA. Why?

IDDY. Well, I thought some special notice would have been taken of the clergy. Reserved seats or something like that. But he treated me as if I were only the organ blower.

SIR CHARLES. There are such a lot of priests in the world, Iddy. It would be impossible to reserve seats for them all.

IDDY. Oh, I meant only the clergy of the Church of England, of course.

MRS HYERING. What I cant get over is their sending along just one angel to judge us, as if we didnt matter.

LADY FARWATERS. He actually went away and forgot to judge us.

PRA. I am not so sure of that.

IDDY. Well, are we sheep or goats? tell me that.

MAYA. You are a sheep, Iddy, my sweet: there can be no doubt about that.

IDDY [*bursting into tears*] I love you, Maya; and you always say unkind things to me. [*He rushes away through the garden, sobbing*].

MAYA. Oh, poor Iddy! I'll go and soothe him with a thousand kisses. [*She runs after him*].

HYERING [*to Sir Charles*] What have you got there? Any news from London?

SIR CHARLES. Yes: Exchange Telegraph and Reuters. Copyright reserved.

HYERING. Lets have it.

SIR CHARLES [*reading*] "Judgment Day. Widespread incredulity as to anything having really happened. Reported appearance of angels in several quarters generally disbelieved. Several witnesses are qualifying or withdrawing their statements in deference to the prevailing scepticism."

HYERING. We shall have to be careful too, Charles. Who will believe us if we tell this yarn of an angel flying down into the garden?

SIR CHARLES. I suppose so. I never thought of it in that way. Still, listen to this. [*Reading*] "Policeman who attempted to arrest angel in Leicester Square removed to mental hospital. Church Assembly at Lambeth Palace decides by a large majority that there has been a Visitation. Dissenting minority, led by the Bishop of Edgbaston, denounces the reports as nonsense that would not impose even on the Society for Psychical Research. His Holiness the Pope warns Christendom that supernatural communications reaching the earth otherwise than through the Church are contrary to the Catholic faith, and, if authentic, must be regarded as demoniacal. Cabinet hastily summoned to discuss the situation. Prime Minister, speaking in emergency meeting at the Mansion House, declares that reports of utterances by angels are hopelessly contradictory, and that alleged verbatim reports by shorthand writers contain vulgar expressions. The Government could not in any case allow the British Empire to be placed in the position of being judged by a commission of a few angels instead of by direct divine authority. Such a slight to the flag would never be tolerated by Englishmen; and the Cabinet was unanimous in refusing to believe that such an outrage had occurred. The Prime Minister's speech was received with thunderous applause, the audience rising spontaneously to sing the National Anthem."

PRA. They would.

SIR CHARLES [*looking at another paper*] Hallo! Whats this? [*Reading*] "Later. During the singing of the second verse of the National Anthem at the Mansion House the proceedings were interrupted by the appearance of an angel with a flaming sword who demanded truculently what they meant by ordering God about to do their dirty political work. He was accompanied by unruly cherubim who floated about tweaking the Lord Mayor's nose, pouring ink into the Prime Minister's hat, and singing derisively Con-Found Their Poll-It-Ticks. Part of the audience fell to their knees, repeating the Confession. Others rushed frantically to the doors. Two Salvation lasses stemmed the rush, at great personal danger to themselves, by standing in the doorway and singing Let Angels Prostrate Fall. Order was restored by the Prime Minister, who offered the angel an unreserved apology and an undertaking that the offending verse should not be sung again. A new one is to be provided by the Poet Laureate. The Premier's last words were lost through the misconduct of a cherub who butted him violently in the solar plexus. A wave of the angel's sword and a terrible thunderclap then threw the entire audience prone to the floor. When they rose to their feet the angel and the cherubs had disappeared."

HYERING. Oh, an invention. We cant swallow those cherubs, really.

SIR CHARLES [*taking up a third paper*] This sounds a little more plausible. "A representative of the Fascist Press has called at the War Office to ask whether any steps are being taken to defend the right of public meeting, and to deal with the angelic peril. The Commander-in-Chief, whilst denying that there is any such thing as a right of public meeting by undisciplined and irresponsible persons, declared that the Mansion House incident was quite incomprehensible to him, as he could not conceive how the only really practical part of the National Anthem could give any offence. Any suggestion that it was not the plain duty of the Ruler of the Universe to confound England's enemies could only lead to widespread atheism. The First Lord of the Admiralty, interviewed last night, said that he could not make head or tail of the reports, but that he could assure the public that whatever had really happened, the British Navy would not take it lying down. Later. A Hyde Park orator was thrown into the Serpentine for saying that the British Empire was not the only pebble on the beach. He has been fined thirty shillings for being in unlawful possession of a life buoy, the property of the Royal Humane Society. There can be no doubt that the disparaging remarks and assumed superiority of the angels has started a wave of patriotism throughout the country which is bound to lead to action of some sort."

PRA. Which means, if it means anything, that England's next war will be a war with heaven.

PROLA. Nothing new in that. England has been at war with heaven for many a long year.

VASHTI [*inspired*] The most splendid of all her wars!

KANCHIN. The last conquest left to her to achieve!

VASHTI. To overcome the angels!

JANGA. To plant the flag of England on the ramparts of Heaven itself! that is the final glory.

PROLA. Oh go away, children: go away. Now that Maya has gone to kiss somebody, there is nothing left for you to glorify but suicide.

VASHTI [*rising*] I rebel.

JANGA [*rising*] We rebel against Prola, the goddess empress.

KANCHIN [*rising*] Prola has turned back from the forlorn hope.

VASHTI. Prola is a coward. She fears defeat and death.

KANCHIN. Without death there can be no heroism.

JANGA. Without faith unto death there can be no faith.

VASHTI. Prola has failed us in the great Day of Judgment.

KANCHIN. Our souls have been called to their final account.

ALL THREE [*marching away through the garden*] Guilty, Prola:

73

guilty. Adieu, Prola!

PROLA. Oh, adieu until you all want your tea.

PRA. We have taught them everything except common sense.

LADY FARWATERS. We have taught them everything except how to work for their daily bread instead of praying for it.

PROLA. It is dangerous to educate fools.

PRA. It is still more dangerous to leave them uneducated.

MRS HYERING. There just shouldnt be any fools. They wernt born fools: we made fools of them.

PRA. We must stop making fools.

Iddy returns alone. Something strange has happened to him. He stares at them and tries to speak; but no sound comes from his lips.

LADY FARWATERS. What on earth is the matter with you, Iddy? Have you been drinking?

IDDY [*in a ghastly voice*] Maya.

PROLA. What has happened to Maya?

IDDY. Heaven and earth shall pass away; but I shall not pass away. That is what she said. And then there was nothing in my arms. Nothing. Nothing in my arms. Heaven and earth would pass away; but the love of Maya would never pass away. And there was nothing. [*He collapses on the well parapet, overcome, not in tears but in a profound awe*].

PRA. Do you mean that she died in your arms?

IDDY. Died? No. I tell you there was nothing. Dont you understand? Where she had just been there was nothing. There never had been anything.

PROLA. And the others? Quick, Pra: go and find the others.

PRA. What others?

PROLA. The other three: our children. I forget their names.

IDDY. They said "Our names shall live forever." What were their names?

HYERING. They have gone clean out of my head.

SIR CHARLES. Most extraordinary. I cant for the life of me remember. How many of them did you say there were, Prola?

PROLA. Four. Or was it four hundred?

IDDY. There were four. Their names were Love, Pride, Heroism and Empire. Love's pet name was Maya. I loved Maya. I loved them all; but it was through love of Maya that I loved them. I held Maya in my arms. She promised to endure for ever; and suddenly there was nothing in my arms. I have searched for the others; but she and they were one: I found nothing. It is the Judgment.

PROLA. Has she left a great void in your heart, Iddy, that girl who turned to nothing in your arms?

IDDY. No. This is a beautiful climate; and you are beautiful people; but you are not real to me; and the sun here is not what it is in the valley of the Severn. I am glad I am an English clergyman. A village and a cottage: a garden and a church: these things will not turn to nothing. I shall be content with my little black coat and my little white collar and my little treasure of words spoken by my Lord Jesus. Blessed be the name of the Lord: I shall not forget it as I shall forget Maya's. [*He goes out seaward like a man in a trance*].

LADY FARWATERS [*troubled, half rising*] But, Iddy,—

PROLA. Let him go. The pigeon knows its way home.

Lady Farwaters sinks back into her seat. There is a moment of rather solemn silence. Then the telephone rings.

PRA [*taking up the receiver*] Yes? . . . What? . . . Yes: amazing news: we know all about that. What is the latest? . . . Yes: "plot to destroy our most valuable citizens": I got that; but what was the first word? What plot? . . . Oh, Russian plot. Rubbish! havnt you some sensible reports? . . . Special news broadcast just coming in? . . . Good: put me on to it. [*To the others*] Im through to London Regional. Listen: I'll repeat it as it comes. [*He echoes the news*] Extraordinary disappearances. Indescribable panic. Stock Exchange closes: only two members left. House of Commons decimated: only fourteen members to be found: none of Cabinet rank. House of Lords still musters fifty members; but not one of them has ever attended a meeting of the Chamber. Mayfair a desert: six hotels left without a single guest. Fresh disappearances. Crowded intercession service at Westminster Abbey brought to a close by disappearance of the congregation at such a rate that the rest fled leaving the dean preaching to the choir. At the Royal Institution Sir Ruthless Bonehead, Egregious Professor of Mechanistic Biology to the Rockefeller Foundation, drew a crowded audience to hear his address on "Whither have they gone?" He disappeared as he opened his mouth to speak. Noted Cambridge professor suggests that what is happening is a weeding-out of nonentities. He has been deprived of his Chair; and The Times, in a leading article, points out that the extreme gravity of the situation lies in the fact that not only is it our most important people who are vanishing, but that it is the most unquestionably useful and popular professions that are most heavily attacked, the medical profession having disappeared almost en bloc, whilst the lawyers and clergy are comparatively immune. A situation of terrible suspense has been created everywhere. Happy husbands and fathers disappear from the family dinner with the soup. Several popular leaders of fashion and famous beauties, after ringing their bells for their maids, have been found non-existent when the bells were answered. More than a million persons have disappeared in the act of reading novels. The Morning Post contains an eloquent protest by Lady Gushing, president of the Titled Ladies' League of Social Service, on the inequality of sacrifice as between the west end and the east, where casualties have been comparatively few. Lady Gushing has since disappeared. There is general agreement that our losses are irreparable, though their bad effects are as yet unfelt. But before long—

HYERING. Whats the use of going on, Pra? The angels are weeding the garden. The useless people, the mischievous people, the selfish somebodies and the noisy nobodies, are dissolving into space, which is the simplest form of matter. We here are awaiting our own doom.

MRS HYERING. What was it the angel said?

PROLA. The lives which have no use, no meaning, no purpose, will fade out. We shall have to justify our existences or perish. We shall live under a constant sense of that responsibility. If the angels fail us we shall set up tribunals of our own from which worthless people will not come out alive. When men no longer fear the judgment of God, they must learn to judge themselves.

SIR CHARLES. I seem to remember somebody saying "Judge not, that ye be not judged."

PROLA. That means "Punish not, that ye be not punished." This is not punishment, but judgment.

HYERING. What is judgment?

PRA. Judgment is valuation. Civilizations live by their valuations. If the valuations are false, the civilization perishes as all the ancient ones we know of did. We are not being punished today: we are being valued. That is the Newest Dispensation.

LADY FARWATERS. I feel an absolute conviction that I shall not disappear and that Charles will not disappear. We have done some queer things here in the east perhaps; but at bottom we are comfortable commonsense probable English people; and we shall not do anything so improbable as disappear.

SIR CHARLES [to his wife] Do not tempt the angels, my dear. Remember: you used to distribute tracts before you met Pra.

LADY FARWATERS. Ssh-sh-sh! Dont remind the angels of those tracts.

HYERING [rising] Look here. I have an uneasy feeling that we'd better get back to our work. I feel pretty sure that we shant disappear as long as we're doing something useful; but if we only sit here talking, either we shall disappear or the people who are listening to us will. What we have learnt here today is that the day of judgment is not the end of the world but the beginning of real human responsibility. Charles and I have still our duties: the Unexpected Islands have to be governed today just as they had to be yesterday. Sally: if you have given your orders for the housework today, go and cook something or sew something or tidy up the books. Come on, Charles. Lets get to work. [He goes into the house].

SIR CHARLES [to his wife, rising] You might take a turn in the garden, dear: gardening is the only unquestionably useful job. [He follows Hyering into the house].

LADY FARWATERS [rising] Prola: shall I bring you some knit-

77

ting to occupy you?

PROLA. No, thank you. I have some thinking to do.

LADY FARWATERS. Well, dear: I hope that will count as work. I shall feel safer with my gardening basket. [*She goes into the house*].

MRS HYERING. J'you think itll be all right if I go and do some crossword puzzles? It cultivates the mind so, dont you think?

PROLA. Does it? Well, do the puzzles and see what will happen. Let life come to you. Goodbye.

MRS HYERING [*alarmed*] Why do you say goodbye? Do you think I am going to disappear?

PROLA. Possibly. Or possibly *I* may.

MRS HYERING. Oh then for heaven's sake dont do it in my presence. Wait til Ive gone.

She scuttles up the steps into the house, leaving Prola and Pra alone together.

PRA. Tell me the truth, Prola. Are you waiting for me to disappear? Do you feel that you can do better without me? Have you always felt that you could do better without me?

PROLA. That is a murderer's thought. Have you ever let yourself think it? How often have you said to yourself "I could do better alone, or with another woman"?

PRA. Fairly often, my dear, when we were younger. But I did not murder you. Thats the answer. And you?

PROLA. All that stuff belongs to the past: to the childhood of our marriage. We have now grown together until we are each of us a part of the other. I no longer think of you as a separate possibility.

PRA. I know. I am part of the furniture of your house. I am a matter of course. But was I always that? Was I that in the childhood of our marriage?

PROLA. You are still young enough and manlike enough to ask mischievous questions.

PRA. No matter: we shall both disappear presently; and I have still some curiosity left. Did you ever really care for me? I know I began as a passion and have ended as a habit, like all husbands;

78

but outside that routine there is a life of the intellect that is quite independent of it. What have I been to you in that life? A help or a hindrance?

PROLA. Pra: I always knew from the very beginning that you were an extraordinarily clever fool.

PRA. Good. That is exactly what I am.

PROLA. But I knew also that nobody but a fool would be frivolous enough to join me in doing all the mad things I wanted to do. And no ordinary fool would have been subtle enough to understand me, nor clever enough to keep off the rocks of social ruin. Ive grown fond enough of you for all practical purposes;—

PRA. Thank you.

PROLA. —but Ive never allowed you or any other man to cut me off my own stem and make me a parasite on his. That sort of love and sacrifice is not the consummation of a capable woman's existence: it is the temptation she must resist at all costs.

PRA. That temptation lies in the man's path too. The worst sacrifices I have seen have been those of men's highest careers to women's vulgarities and follies.

PROLA. Well, we two have no reproaches and no regrets on that score.

PRA. No. We are awaiting judgment here quite simply as a union of a madwoman with a fool.

PROLA. Who thought they had created four wonderful children. And who are now brought to judgment and convicted of having created nothing. We have only repeated the story of Helen and Faust and their beautiful child Euphorion. Euphorion also vanished, in his highest flight.

PRA. Yes; but Helen was a dream. You are not a dream. The children did not vanish like Euphorion in their infancy. They grew up to bore me more intensely than I have ever been bored by any other set of human creatures. Come, confess: did they not bore you?

PROLA. Have I denied it? Of course they bored me. They must have bored one another terribly in spite of all their dressing up and pretending that their fairyland was real. How they must have envied the gardener's boy his high spirits!

PRA. The coming race will not be like them. Meanwhile we are face to face with the fact that we two have made a precious mess of our job of producing the coming race by a mixture of east and west. We are failures. We shall disappear.

PROLA. I do not feel like that. I feel like the leader of a cavalry charge whose horse has been shot through the head and dropped dead under him. Well, a dead hobby horse is not the end of the world. Remember: we are in the Unexpected Isles; and in the Unexpected Isles all plans fail. So much the better: plans are only jigsaw puzzles: one gets tired of them long before one can piece them together. There are still a million lives beyond all the Utopias and the Millenniums and the rest of the jigsaw puzzles: I am a woman and I know it. Let men despair and become cynics and pessimists because in the Unexpected Isles all their little plans fail: women will never let go their hold on life. We are not here to fulfil prophecies and fit ourselves into puzzles, but to wrestle with life as it comes. And it never comes as we expect it to come.

PRA. It comes like a thief in the night.

PROLA. Or like a lover. Never will Prola go back to the Country of the Expected.

PRA. There is no Country of the Expected. The Unexpected Isles are the whole world.

PROLA. Yes, if our fools only had vision enough to see that. I tell you this is a world of miracles, not of jigsaw puzzles. For me every day must have its miracle, and no child be born like any child that ever was born before. And to witness this miracle of the children I will abide the uttermost evil and carry through it the seed of the uttermost good.

PRA. Then I, Pra, must continue to strive for more knowledge and more power, though the new knowledge always contradicts the old, and the new power is the destruction of the fools who misuse it.

PROLA. We shall plan commonwealths when our empires have brought us to the brink of destruction; but our plans will still lead us to the Unexpected Isles. We shall make wars because only under the strain of war are we capable of changing the world; but the changes our wars will make will never be the changes we intended them to make. We shall clamor for security like frightened children; but in the Unexpected Isles there is no security; and the future is to those who prefer surprise and wonder to security. I, Prola, shall live and grow because surprise and wonder are the very breath of my being, and routine is death to me. Let every day be a day of wonder for me and I shall not fear the Day of Judgment. [*She is interrupted by a roll of thunder*]. Be silent: you cannot frighten Prola with stage thunder. The fountain of life is within me.

PRA. But you have given the key of it to me, the Man.

PROLA. Yes: I need you and you need me. Life needs us both.

PRA. All hail, then, the life to come!

PROLA. All Hail. Let it come.

They pat hands, eastern fashion.

THE SIX OF CALAIS

XLVI

1934

PREFATORY TO THE SIX OF CALAIS

THE most amusing thing about the first performance of this little play was the exposure it elicited of the quaint illiteracy of our modern London journalists. Their only notion of a king was a pleasant and highly respectable gentleman in a bowler hat and Victorian beard, shaking hands affably with a blushing football team. To them a queen was a dignified lady, also Victorian as to her coiffure, graciously receiving bouquets from excessively washed children in beautiful new clothes. Such were their mental pictures of Great Edward's grandson and his queen Philippa. They were hurt, shocked, scandalized at the spectacle of a medieval soldier-monarch publicly raging and cursing, crying and laughing, asserting his authority with thrasonic ferocity and the next moment blubbering like a child in his wife's lap or snarling like a savage dog at a dauntless and defiant tradesman: in short, behaving himself like an unrestrained human being in a very trying situation instead of like a modern constitutional monarch on parade keeping up an elaborate fiction of living in a political vacuum and moving only when his ministers pull his strings. Edward Plantagenet the Third had to pull everybody else's strings and pull them pretty hard, his father having been miserably killed for taking his job too lightly. But the journalist critics knew nothing of this. A King Edward who did not behave like the son of King Edward the Seventh seemed unnatural and indecent to them, and they rent their garments accordingly.

They were perhaps puzzled by the fact that the play has no moral whatever. Every year or so I hurl at them a long play full of insidious propaganda, with a moral in every line. They never discover what I am driving at: it is always too plainly and domestically stated to be grasped by their subtle and far flung minds; but they feel that I am driving at something: probably something they had better not agree with if they value their livelihoods. A play of mine in which I am not driving at anything more than a playwright's direct business is as inconceivable by them as a medieval king.

Now a playwright's direct business is simply to provide the theatre with a play. When I write one with the additional attraction of providing the twentieth century with an up-to-date religion or the like, that luxury is thrown in gratuitously; and the play, simply as a play, is not necessarily either the better or the worse for it. What, then, is a play simply as a play?

Well, it is a lot of things. Life as we see it is so haphazard that it is only by picking out its key situations and arranging them in their significant order (which is never how they actually occur) that it can be made intelligible. The highbrowed dramatic poet wants to make it intelligible and sublime. The farce writer wants to make it funny. The melodrama merchant wants to make it as exciting as some people find the police news. The pornographer wants to make it salacious. All interpreters of life in action, noble or ignoble, find their instrument in the theatre; and all the academic definitions of a play are variations of this basic function.

Yet there is one function hardly ever alluded to now, though it was made much too much of from Shakespear's time to the middle of the nineteenth century. As I write my plays it is continually in my mind and very much to my taste. This function is to provide an exhibition of the art of acting. A good play with bad parts is not an impossibility; but it is a monstrosity. A bad play with good parts will hold the stage and be kept alive by the actors for centuries after the obsolescence of its mentality would have condemned it to death without them. A great deal of the British Drama, from Shakespear to Bulwer Lytton, is as dead as mutton, and quite unbearable except when heroically acted; yet Othello and Richelieu can still draw hard money into the pay boxes; and The School For Scandal revives again and again with unabated vigor. Rosalind can always pull As You Like It through in spite of the sententious futility of the melancholy Jaques; and Millamant, impossible as she is, still produces the usual compliments to the wit and style of Congreve, who thought that syphilis and cuckoldry and concupiscent old women are things to be laughed at.

PREFATORY TO THE SIX OF CALAIS

The Six of Calais is an acting piece and nothing else. As it happened, it was so well acted that in the eighteenth century all the talk would have been about Siddons as Philippa. But the company got no thanks except from the audience: the critics were prostrated with shock, damn their eyes!

I have had to improve considerably on the story as told by that absurd old snob Froissart, who believed that "to rob and pill was a good life" if the robber was at least a baron. He made a very poor job of it in my opinion.

ON THE HIGH SEAS,
  28th May 1935.

NOTE. The Six of Calais was performed for the first time in Mr. Sydney Carroll's Open Air Theatre, in Regent's Park, London, on the 17th July 1934, with Phyllis Neilson Terry, Charles Carson, Leonard Shepherd, and Vincent Sternroyd in the four principal parts.

THE SIX OF CALAIS

A.D. 4th August 1347. Before the walls of Calais on the last day of the siege. The pavilion of Edward III, King of England, is on your left as you face the walls. The pavilion of his consort Philippa of Hainault is on your right. Between them, near the King's pavilion, is a two-seated chair of state for public audiences. Crowds of tents cover the background; but there is a clear way in the middle through the camp to the great gate of the city with its drawbridge still up and its flag still flying.

The Black Prince, aged 17, arrives impetuously past the Queen's tent, a groom running after him.

THE PRINCE. Here is the King's pavilion without a single attendant to announce me. What can the matter be?

A child's scream is heard from the royal pavilion; and John of Gaunt, aged 7, dashes out and is making for his mother's tent when the Prince seizes him.

THE PRINCE. How now, Johnny? Whats the matter?

JOHN [*struggling*] Let me go. Father is in a frightful wax.

THE PRINCE. I shall be in a wax myself presently. [*Releasing him*] Off with you to mother. [*The child takes refuge in the Queen's pavilion*].

THE KING'S VOICE. Grrr! Yah! Why was I not told? Gogswoons, why was I not told? [*Edward III, aged 35, dashes from his pavilion, foaming*]. Out! [*The groom flies for his life*]. How long have you been here? They never tell me anything. I might be a dog instead of a king.

THE PRINCE [*about to kneel*] Majesty—

THE KING. No no: enough of that. Your news. Anything from Scotland? Anything from Wales?

THE PRINCE. I—

THE KING [*not waiting for the answer*] The state of things here is past words. The wrath of God and all his saints is upon this expedition.

THE PRINCE. I hope not, sir. I—

THE KING [*raging on*] May God wither and blast this accursed town! You would have thought that these dogs would have come out of their kennels and grovelled for mercy at my summons. Am I not their lawful king, ha?

THE PRINCE. Undoubtedly, sir. They—

THE KING. They have held me up for twelve months! A whole year!! My business ruined! My plans upset! My money exhausted! Death, disease, mutiny, a dog's life here in the field winter and summer. The bitch's bastard who is in command of their walls came to demand terms from me! to demand terms!!! looked me straight in the eyes with his head up as if I—I, his king! were dirt beneath his feet. By God, I will have that head: I will kick it to my dogs to eat. I will chop his insolent herald into four quarters—

THE PRINCE [*shocked*] Oh no, sir: not a herald: you cannot do that.

THE KING. They have driven me to such extremity that I am capable of cutting all the heralds in Christendom into their quarterings. [*He sits down in his chair of state and suddenly becomes ridiculously sentimental*]. I have not told you the worst. Your mother, the Queen, my Philippa, is here: here! Edward, in her delicate state of health. Even that did not move them. They want her to die: they are trying to murder her and our innocent unborn child. Think of that, boy: oh, think of that [*he almost weeps*].

THE PRINCE. Softly, father: that is not their fault: it is yours.

THE KING. Would you make a jest of this? If it is not their fault it shall be their misfortune; for I will have every man, woman, and child torn to pieces with red hot pincers for it.

THE PRINCE. Truly, dear Sir, you have great cause to be annoyed; but in sober earnest how does the matter stand? They must be suffering the last extremity of famine. Their walls may hold out; but their stomachs cannot. Cannot you offer them some sort of terms to end the business? Money is running short. Time is running short. You only make them more desperate by threatening them. Remember: it is good policy to build a bridge of silver for a flying foe.

THE KING. Do I not know it? Have I not been kind, magnanimous? Have I not done all that Christian chivalry could require of me? And they abuse my kindness: it only encourages them: they despise me for it.

THE PRINCE. What terms have you offered them?

THE KING. I have not threatened the life of a single knight. I have said that no man of gentle condition and noble blood shall be denied quarter and ransom. It was their knightly duty to make a show of arms against me. But [*rising wrathfully*] these base rascals of burgesses: these huckstering hounds of merchants who have made this port of Calais a nest of pirates: these usurers and tradesmen: these rebel curs who have dared to take up arms against their betters: am I to pardon their presumption? I should be false to our order, to Christendom, if I did not make a signal example.

THE PRINCE. By all means, sir. But what have you demanded?

THE KING. Six of the most purseproud of their burgesses, as they call themselves—by God, they begin to give themselves the airs of barons—six of them are to come in their shirts with halters round their necks for me to hang in the sight of all their people. [*Raising his voice again and storming*] They shall die the dog's death they deserve. They shall—

A court lady comes in.

THE COURT LADY. Sir: the Queen. Sssh!

THE KING [*subsiding to a whisper*] The Queen! Boy: not a word here. Her condition: she must not be upset: she takes these things so amiss: be discreet, for heaven's sake.

Queen Philippa, aged 33, comes from her pavilion, attended.

THE QUEEN. Dear child: welcome.

THE PRINCE. How do you, lady mother? [*He kisses her hand*].

THE KING [*solicitously*] Madam: are you well wrapped up? Is it wise to come into the cold air here? Had they better not bring a brazier and some cushions, and a hot drink—a posset—

THE QUEEN [*curtseying*] Sir: beloved: dont fuss. I am very well; and the air does me good. [*To the Prince*] You must cheer up your father, my precious. He will fret about my health when it is his own that needs care. I have borne him eleven children; and St Anne be my witness they have cost less looking after than this one big soldier, the greatest baby of them all. [*To the King*] Have you put on your flannel belly band, dearest?

THE KING. Yes, yes, yes, my love: do not bother about me. Think of yourself and our child—

THE QUEEN. Oh, leave me to take care of myself and the child. I am no maternal malingreuse I promise you. And now, sir sonny, tell me all your news. I—

She is interrupted by a shrill trumpet call.

THE KING. What is that? What now?

John of Gaunt, who has been up to the town gates to see the fun, runs in excitedly.

JOHN OF GAUNT [*bending his knee very perfunctorily*] Sire: they have surrendered: the drawbridge is down. The six old men have come out in their shirts with ropes round their necks.

THE KING [*clouting him*] Sssh! Hold your tongue, you young devil.

THE QUEEN. Old men in their shirts in this weather!! They will catch cold.

THE KING. It is nothing, madam my love: only the ceremony of surrender. You must go in: it is not fitting that these half naked men should be in your presence. I will deal with them.

THE QUEEN. Do not keep them too long in the cold, dearest sir.

THE KING [*uxoriously waving her a kiss*] My love!

The Queen goes into her pavilion; and a group of noblemen attendant on the King, including Sir Walter Manny and the Lords Derby, Northampton, and Arundel, issue from their tents and assemble behind the chair of state, where they are joined by the Black Prince, who stands at the King's right hand and takes charge of John of Gaunt.

THE KING. Now for these swine, these bloodsuckers. They shall learn—[*shouting*] Fetch me these fellows in here. Drag them in. I'll teach them to hold me up here for twelve months. I'll—

The six burgesses, hustled by men-at-arms, enter in their shirts and halters, each carrying a bunch of massive iron keys. Their leader, Eustache de St Pierre, kneels at the King's feet. Four of his fellow victims, Piers de Wissant, Jacques de Wissant, Jean d'Aire, and Gilles d'Oudebolle, kneel in pairs behind him, and, following his example, lay their keys on the ground. They are deeply cast down, bearing themselves like condemned men, yet maintaining a melancholy dignity. Not so the sixth, Piers de Rosty (nicknamed Hardmouth), the only one without a grey or white beard. He has an extraordinarily dogged chin with a few bristles on it. He deliberately separates himself from the rest by passing behind the royal chair to the King's right and planting himself stiffly erect in an attitude of intense recalcitrance. The King, scowling fiercely at St Pierre and the rest, does not notice this until Peter flings down his keys with a violence which suggests that he would very willingly have brained Edward with them.

THE KING. On your knees, hound.

PETER. I am a good dog, but not of your kennel, Neddy.

THE KING. Neddy!!!!

PETER. Order your own curs: I am a free burgess and take commands from nobody.

Before the amazed monarch can retort, Eustache appeals to Peter.

EUSTACHE. Master Peter: if you have no regard for yourself, remember that our people, our wives and children, are at the mercy of this great king.

PETER. You mistake him for his grandfather. Great! [*He spits*].

EUSTACHE. Is this your promise to be patient?

PETER. Why waste civilities on him, Master Mayor? He can do no worse than hang us; and as to the town, *I* would have burnt it to the last brick, and every man, woman and child along with it, sooner than surrender. I came here to make up the tale of six to be hanged. Well, he can hang me; but he shall not outface me. I am as good a dog as he, any day in the week.

THE PRINCE. Fie, fellow! is this a way for one of thy degree to speak to an anointed king? Bear thyself as befits one of thy degree in the royal presence, or by Holy Paul—

PETER. You know how we have borne ourselves in his royal

presence these twelve months. We have made some of you skip. Famine and not you, has beaten us. Give me a square meal and a good sword and stake all on a fair single combat with this big bully, or his black whelp here if he is afraid of me; and we shall see which is the better dog of the two.

THE KING. Drag him to his knees. Hamstring him if he resists.

Three men-at-arms dash at Peter and drag him to his knees. They take his halter and tie his ankles and wrists with it. Then they fling him on his side, where he lies helpless.

THE KING. And so, Master Burgess—

PETER. Bow-wow-wow!

THE KING [*furious*] Gag him. Gogswoons, gag him.

They tear a piece of linen from the back of his shirt, and bind his mouth with it. He barks to the last moment. John of Gaunt laughs ecstatically at this performance, and sets off some of the soldiers.

THE KING. If a man laughs I will have him flayed alive.

Dead silence.

THE KING. And now, fellows, what have ye to say to excuse your hardy and stubborn resistance for all these months to me, your king?

EUSTACHE. Sir, we are not fellows. We are free burgesses of this great city.

THE KING. Free burgesses! Are you still singing that song? Well, I will bend the necks of your burgesses when the hangman has broken yours. Am I not your overlord? Am I not your anointed king?

EUSTACHE. That is your claim, sir; and you have made it good by force of arms. We must submit to you and to God.

THE KING. Leave God out of this! What hast thou or thy like to do with God?

EUSTACHE. Nothing, sir: we would not so far presume. But with due respect to your greatness I would humbly submit to your Majesty that God may have something to do with us, seeing that he created us all alike and redeemed us by the blood of his beloved son.

THE KING [*to the Prince*] Can you make head or tail of this, boy? Is he accusing me of impiety? If he is, by God—

EUSTACHE. Sir, is it for me to accuse you of anything? Here we kneel in the dust before you, naked and with the ropes on our necks with which you will presently send us into the presence of our maker and yours. [*His teeth chatter*].

THE KING. Ay: you may well tremble. You have cause.

EUSTACHE. Yes: I tremble; and my teeth chatter: the few I have left. But you gentlemen that see our miserable plight, I call on your generosity as noblemen, on your chivalry as good knights, to bear witness for us that it is the cold of the morning and our naked condition that shakes us. We kneel to implore your King's mercy for our wretched and starving townsfolk, not for ourselves.

THE KING. Whose fault is it that they are starving? They have themselves to thank. Why did they not open their gates to me? Why did they take arms against their anointed king? Why should I have mercy on them or on you?

EUSTACHE. Sir: one is merciful not for reasons, but for the love of God, at whose hand we must all sue for mercy at the end of our days.

THE KING. You shall not save yourself by preaching. What right have you to preach? It is for churchmen and learned divines to speak of these mysteries, not for tradesmen and usurers. I'll teach you to rebel against your betters, whom God has appointed to keep you in obedience and loyalty. You are traitors; and as traitors you shall die. Thank my mercy that you are spared the torments that traitors and rebels suffer in England. [*Rising*] Away with them to the hangman; and let our trumpeters summon the towns-people to the walls to take warning from their dangling corpses.

The three men-at-arms begin to lift Peter. The others lay hands on his five colleagues.

THE KING. No: let that hound lie. Hanging is too good for him.

The Queen hurries in with her ladies in great concern. The men-at-arms release the burgesses irresolutely. It is evident that the Queen's arrival washes out all the King's orders.

THE QUEEN. Sir, what is this they tell me?

THE KING [*hurrying across to intercept her*] Madam: this is no place for you. I pray you, retire. The business is one in which it becomes you not to meddle.

THE QUEEN [*evading him and passing on to inspect the burgesses*] But these gentlemen. They are almost naked. It is neither seemly nor sufficient. They are old: they are half frozen: they should be in their beds.

THE KING. They soon will be. Leave us, madam. This is business of State. They are suffering no more than they deserve. I beg and pray you—I command you—

THE QUEEN. Dear sir, your wishes are my law and your commands my duty. But these gentlemen are very cold.

THE KING. They will be colder presently; so you need not trouble about that. Will it please you, madam, to withdraw at once?

THE QUEEN. Instantly, my dear lord. [*To Eustache*] Sir: when his Majesty has ended his business with you, will you and your friends partake of some cups of hot wine in my pavilion? You shall be furnished with gowns.

THE KING [*choking with wrath*] Hot w—!

EUSTACHE. Alas, madam, when the King has ended his business with us we shall need nothing but our coffins. I also beg you to withdraw and hasten our despatch to that court where we shall not be held guilty for defending our hearths and homes to the last extremity. The King will not be baulked of his revenge; and we are shriven and ready.

THE QUEEN. Oh, you mistake, sir: the King is incapable of revenge: my husband is the flower of chivalry.

EUSTACHE. You little know your husband, madam. We know better what to expect from Edward Plantagenet.

THE KING [*coming to him threateningly past his consort*] Ha! do you, Master Merchant? You know better than the Queen! You and your like know what to expect from your lords and rulers! Well, this time you shall not be disappointed. You have guessed aright. You shall hang, every man of you, in your shirts, to make mirth for my horseboys and their trulls.

THE QUEEN. Oh no—

THE KING [*thundering*] Madam: I forbid you to speak. I bade you go: you would not; and now you shall see what I would have spared you had you been obedient. By God, I will be master in my own house and king in my own camp. Take these fellows out and hang them in their white beards.

The King takes his place on his chair of state with his arms folded implacably. The Queen follows him slowly and desolately. She takes her place beside him. The dead silence is very trying.

THE QUEEN [*drooping in tears and covering her face with her hands*] Oh!

THE KING [*flinching*] No no no no NO. Take her away.

THE QUEEN. Sir: I have been always a great trouble to you. I have asked you for a thousand favors and graces and presents. I am impatient and ungrateful, ever asking, asking, asking. Have you ever refused me even once?

THE KING. Well, is that a reason why I should give and grant, grant and give, for ever? Am I never to have my own way?

THE QUEEN. Oh, dearest sir, when next I ask you for a great thing, refuse me: teach me a lesson. But this is such a little thing. [*Heartbroken*] I cannot bear your refusing me a little thing.

THE KING. A little thing! You call this a little thing!

THE QUEEN. A very very little thing, sir. You are the King: you have at your disposal thousands of lives: all our lives from the noblest to the meanest. All the lives in that city are in your hand to do as you will with in this your hour of victory: it is as if you were God himself. You said once that you would lead ten kings captive to my feet. Much as I have begged from you I have never asked for my ten kings. I ask only for six old merchants, men beneath your royal notice, as my share of the spoils of your conquest. Their ransom will hardly buy me a new girdle; and oh, dear sir, you know that my old one is becoming too strait for me. Will you keep me begging so?

THE KING. I see very well that I shall not be allowed my own way. [*He begins to cry*].

THE QUEEN [*throwing her arms round him*] Oh, dear sir, you

97   H

know I would die to spare you a moment's distress. There, there, dearest! [*She pets him*].

THE KING [*blubbering*] I am never allowed to do anything I want. I might as well be a dog as a king. You treat me like a baby.

THE QUEEN. Ah no: you are the greatest of kings to me, the noblest of men, my dearest lord and my dearest dearest love. [*Throwing herself on her knees*] Listen: do as you will: I will not say another word: I ask nothing.

THE KING. No: you ask nothing because you know you will get everything. [*He rises, shouting*] Take those men out of my sight.

THE PRINCE. What shall we do with them, sir?

THE KING [*flinging himself back into his seat*] Ask the Queen. Banquet them: feast them: give them my crown, my kingdom. Give them the clothes off my back, the bread out of my mouth, only take them away. Will you go, curses on you.

The five burgesses kneel gratefully to the Queen.

EUSTACHE [*kissing her hand*] Madam: our ransom shall buy you a threefold girdle of gold and a cradle of silver.

THE KING. Aye, well, see that it does: see that it does.

The burgesses retire, bowing to the Queen, who, still on her knees, waves her hand graciously to them.

THE QUEEN. Will you not help me up, dear sir?

THE KING. Oh yes, yes [*raising her*]: you should be more careful: who knows what harm you may have done yourself flopping on your knees like that?

THE QUEEN. I have done myself no harm, dear sir; but you have done me a world of good. I have never been better nor happier in my life. Look at me. Do I not look radiant?

THE KING. And how do I look? Like a fool.

JOHN OF GAUNT. Sir: the men-at-arms want to know what they are to do with this fellow?

THE KING. Aye, I forgot him. Fetch him here.

The three men-at-arms carry Peter to the King, and fling him down. The King is now grinning. His paroxysm of tears has com-

pletely discharged his ill temper. It dawns on him that through Peter he may get even with Philippa for his recent domestic defeat.

THE QUEEN. Oh, the poor man has not even a proper shirt to wear. It is all torn: it is hardly decent.

THE KING. Look well at this man, madam. He defied me. He spat at me. There is no insult that he did not heap on me. He looked me in the face and spoke to me as if I were a scullion. I swear to you by the Holy Rood, he called me Neddy! Donkeys are called Neddy. What have you to say now? Is he, too, to be spared and petted and fed and have a gown from you?

THE QUEEN [*going to Peter*] But he is blue with cold. I fear he is dying. Untie him. Lift him up. Take that bandage off his mouth. Fie fie! I believe it is the tail of his shirt.

THE KING. It is cleaner than his tongue.

The men-at-arms release Peter from his bonds and his gag. He is too stiff to rise. They pull him to his feet.

PETER [*as they lift him groaning and swearing*] Ah-ooh-oh-ow!

THE KING. Well? Have you learnt your lesson? Are you ready to sue for the Queen's mercy?

PETER. Yah! Henpecked! Kiss mammy!

THE KING [*chuckles*]!!

THE QUEEN [*severely*] Are you mad, Master Burgess? Do you not know that your life is in the King's hand? Do you expect me to recommend you to his mercy if you forget yourself in this unseemly fashion?

PETER. Let me tell you, madam, that I came here in no ragged shirt. I have a dozen shirts of as fine a web as ever went on your back. Is it likely that I, a master mercer, would wear aught but the best of the best to go to my grave in?

THE QUEEN. Mend your manners first, sir; and then mend your linen; or you shall have no countenance from me.

PETER. I have naught to do with you, madam, though I well see who wears the breeches in this royal household. I am not skilled in dealing with fine handsome ladies. Leave me to settle my business with your henpecked husband.

THE QUEEN. You shall suffer for this insolence. [*To the King*]

Will you, my lord, stand by and hear me spoken to in this tone by a haberdasher?

THE KING [*grinning*] Nay: I am in a merciful mood this morning. The poor man is to be pitied, shivering there in his shirt with his tail torn off.

PETER. Shivering! You lie in your teeth, though you were fifty kings. No man alive shall pity Peter Hardmouth, a dog of lousy Champagne.

THE KING [*going to him*] Ha! A dog of Champagne! Oh, you must pardon this man, madam; for my grandmother hailed from that lousy province; so I also am a dog of Champagne. We know one another's bark. [*Turning on him with bristling teeth*] Eh?

PETER [*growling in his face like a dog*] Grrrr!!!

THE KING [*returning the growl chin to chin*] Grrrr!!!!!!

They repeat this performance, to the great scandal of the Queen, until it develops into a startling imitation of a dog fight.

THE QUEEN [*tearing the two dogs asunder*] Oh, for shame, sir! And you, fellow: I will have you muzzled and led through the streets on a chain and lodged in a kennel.

THE KING. Be merciful, lady. I have asked you for many favors, and had them granted me too, as the world, please God, will soon have proof. Will you deny me this?

THE QUEEN. Will you mock my condition before this insolent man and before the world? I will not endure it.

THE KING. Faith, no, dearest: no mockery. But you have no skill in dealing with the dogs of lousy Champagne. We must pity this poor trembling fellow.

THE QUEEN [*angrily*] He is not trembling.

PETER. No, by all the saints in heaven and devils in hell. Well said, lass.

He nudges her, to her extreme indignation.

THE KING. Hear that, dearest: he calls thee lass. Be kind to him. He is only a poor old cur who has lost half his teeth. His condition would move a heart of stone.

PETER. I may be an old cur; but if I had sworn to hang the six of us as he swore, no shrew should scold me out of it, nor any softbosomed beauty wheedle me out of it. Yah, cry baby! Give her your sword and sit in the corner with her distaff. The grey mare is the better horse here. Do your worst, dame: I like your spunk better than his snivel.

THE QUEEN [*raging*] Send him away, sir. He is too ugly; and his words are disgusting. Such objects should be kept out of my sight: would you have me bear you a monster? Take him away.

THE KING. Away with him. Hurt him not; but let him not come into the Queen's presence. Quick there. Off with him.

The men-at-arms lay hands on Peter who struggles violently.

PETER. Hands off me, spaniels. Arrr! Grrr! [*As they drag him out overpowered*] Gee-up, Neddy. [*He finishes with a spirited imitation of a donkey's bray*].

THE KING. That is how they build men in Champagne. By the Holy Rood I care not if a bit of him gets into our baby.

THE QUEEN. Oh, for shame! for shame! Have men no decency?

The King snatches her into his arms, laughing boisterously. The laugh spreads to all the soldiers and courtiers. The whole camp seems in a hilarious uproar.

THE QUEEN. No no: for shame! for shame!

The King stops her mouth with a kiss. Peter brays melodiously in the distance.

THE MILLIONAIRESS

XLVII

1936

PREFACE ON BOSSES

THOUGH this play of The Millionairess does not pretend to be anything more than a comedy of humorous and curious contemporary characters such as Ben Jonson might write were he alive now, yet it raises a question that has troubled human life and moulded human society since the creation.

The law is equal before all of us; but we are not all equal before the law. Virtually there is one law for the rich and another for the poor, one law for the cunning and another for the simple, one law for the forceful and another for the feeble, one law for the ignorant and another for the learned, one law for the brave and another for the timid, and within family limits one law for the parent and no law at all for the child.

In the humblest cabin that contains a family you may find a *maitresse femme* who rules in the household by a sort of divine right. She may rule amiably by being able to think more quickly and see further than the others, or she may be a tyrant ruling violently by intensity of will and ruthless egotism. She may be a grandmother and she may be a girl. But the others find they are unable to resist her. Often of course the domestic tyrant is a man; but the phenomenon is not so remarkable in his case, as he is by convention the master and lawgiver of the hearthstone.

In every business street you will find a shopkeeper who is always in difficulties and ends his business adventures in the bankruptcy court. Hard by you will find another shopkeeper, with no greater advantages to start with, or possibly less, who makes larger and larger profits, and inspires more and more confidence in his banker, until he ends as the millionaire head of a giant multiple shop.

How does the captain of a pirate ship obtain his position and maintain his authority over a crew of scoundrels who are all, like himself, outside the law? How does an obscure village priest, the son of humble fisherfolk, come to wear the triple crown and sit in the papal chair? How do common soldiers become Kings, Shahs, and Dictators? Why does a hereditary peer find that he is a nonentity in a grand house organized and ruled by his butler?

Questions like these force themselves on us so continually and ruthlessly that many turn in despair from Socialism and political reform on the ground that to abolish all the institutional tyrannies would only deliver the country helplessly into the hands of the born bosses. A king, a prelate, a squire, a capitalist, a justice of the peace may be a good kind Christian soul, owing his position, as most of us do, to being the son of his father; but a born boss is one who rides roughshod over us by some mysterious power that separates him from our species and makes us fear him: that is, hate him.

What is to be done with that section of the possessors of specific talents whose talent is for moneymaking? History and daily experience teach us that if the world does not devise some plan of ruling them, they will rule the world. Now it is not desirable that they should rule the world; for the secret of moneymaking is to care for nothing else and to work at nothing else; and as the world's welfare depends on operations by which no individual can make money, whilst its ruin by war and drink and disease and drugs and debauchery is enormously profitable to moneymakers, the supremacy of the moneymaker is the destruction of the State. A society which depends on the incentive of private profit is doomed.

And what about ambitious people who possess commanding business ability or military genius or both? They are irresistible unless they are restrained by law; for ordinary individuals are helpless in their hands. Are they to be the masters of society or its servants?

What should the nineteenth century have done in its youth with Rothschild and Napoleon? What is the United States to do with its money kings and bosses? What are we to do with ours? How is the mediocre private citizen to hold his own with the able bullies and masterful women who establish family despotisms, school despotisms, office despotisms, religious despotisms in their little circles all over the country? Our boasted political liberties are a mockery to the subjects of such despotisms. They may work well when the despot is benevolent; but they are worse than any political tyranny in the selfish cases.

It is much more difficult to attack a personal despotism than an institutional one. Monarchs can be abolished: they have been abolished in all directions during the last century and a half, with the result, however, of sometimes replacing a personally amiable and harmless monarch, reigning under strict constitutional and traditional restraints, by energetic dictators and presidents who, having made hay of constitutions and traditions, are under no restraints at all. A hereditary monarch, on the throne because he is the son of his father, may be a normal person, amenable to reasonable advice from his councils, and exercising no authority except that conferred on him (or her) by the Constitution. Behead him, as we beheaded our Charles, or the French their Louis, and the born despot Cromwell or Napoleon (I purposely avoid glaring contemporary examples because I am not quite sure where they will be by the time this book is published) takes his place. The same mysterious personal force that makes the household tyrant, the school tyrant, the office tyrant, the brigand chief and the pirate captain, brings the born boss to the top by a gravitation that ordinary people cannot resist.

The successful usurpers of thrones are not the worst cases. The political usurper may be an infernal scoundrel, ruthless in murder, treachery, and torture; but once his ambition is achieved and he has to rule a nation, the magnitude and difficulty of his job, and the knowledge that if he makes a mess of it he will fall as suddenly as he has risen, will civilize him with a ruthlessness greater than his own. When Henry IV usurped the English crown he certainly did not intend to die of political overwork; but that is what happened to him. No political ruler could possibly be as wickedly selfish and cruel as the tyrant of a private house. Queen Elizabeth was a *maitresse femme*; but she could have had her own way much more completely as landlady of the Mermaid Tavern than she had as sovereign of England. Because Nero and Paul I of Russia could not be made to understand this, they were killed like mad dogs by their own courtiers. But our petty fireside tyrants are not killed. Christina of Sweden would not have had to abdicate if her realm had been a ten-roomed villa. Had Catherine II reigned over her husband only, she need not nor could not have had him murdered; but as Tsarina she was forced to liquidate poor Peter very much against her own easy good nature, which prevented her from scolding her maids properly.

Modern Liberal democracy claims unlimited opportunities for tyranny: qualification for rule by heredity and class narrows it and puts it in harness and blinkers. Especially does such democracy favor money rule. It is in fact not democracy at all, but unashamed plutocracy. And as the meanest creature can become rich if he devotes his life to it, and the people with wider and more generous interests become or remain poor with equal certainty, plutocracy is the very devil socially, because it creates a sort of Gresham law by which the baser human currency drives out the nobler coinage. This is quite different from the survival of the fittest in the contests of character and talent which are independent of money. If Moses is the only tribesman capable of making a code of laws, he inevitably becomes Lawgiver to all the tribes, and, equally inevitably, is forced to add to what he can understand of divine law a series of secular regulations designed to maintain his personal authority. If he finds that it is useless to expect the tribesmen to obey his laws as a matter of common sense, he must persuade them that his inspiration is the result of direct and miraculous communication with their deity. Moses and Mahomet and Joseph Smith the Mormon had to plead divine revelations to get them out of temporary and personal difficulties as well as out of eternal and impersonal ones. As long as an individual of their calibre remains the indispensable man (or woman) doing things that the common man can neither do without nor do for himself, he will be, up to a point, the master of the common man in spite of all the democratic fudge that may be advanced to the contrary.

Of course there are limits. He cannot go to the lengths at which the common man will believe him to be insane or impious: when measures of that complexion are necessary, as they very often are, he must either conceal them or mask them as follies of the sort the common man thinks splendid. If the ruler thinks it well to begin a world war he must persuade his people that it is a war to end war, and that the people he wants them to kill are diabolical scoundrels; and if he is forced to suspend hostilities for a while, and does so by a treaty which contains the seeds of half a dozen new wars and is impossible enough in its conditions to make its violation certain, he must create a general belief that it is a charter of eternal peace and a monument of retributive justice.

In this way the most honest ruler becomes a tyrant and a fabricator of legends and falsehoods, not out of any devilment in himself, but because those whom he rules do not understand his business, and, if they did, would not sacrifice their own immediate interests to the permanent interests of the nation or the world. In short, a ruler must not only make laws, and rule from day to day: he must, by school instruction and printed propaganda, create and maintain an artificial mentality which will endorse his proceedings and obey his authority. This mentality becomes what we call Conservatism; and the revolt against it when it is abused oppressively or becomes obsolete as social conditions change, is classed as sedition, and reviled as Radicalism, Anarchism, Bolshevism, or what you please.

When a mentality is created and a code imposed, the born ruler, the Moses or Lenin, is no longer indispensable: routine government by dunderheads becomes possible and in fact preferable as long as the routine is fairly appropriate to the current phase of social development. The assumption of the more advanced spirits that revolutionists are always right is as questionable as the conservative assumption that they are always wrong. The industrious dunderhead who always does what was done last time because he is incapable of conceiving anything better, makes the best routineer. This explains the enormous part played by dunderheads as such in the history of all nations, provoking repeated explanations of surprise at the littleness of the wisdom with which the world is governed.

But what of the ambitious usurper? the person who has a

capacity for kingship but has no kingdom and must therefore
acquire a readymade one which is getting along in its own way
very well without him? It cannot be contended with any plausi-
bility that William the Conqueror was indispensable in England:
he wanted England and grabbed it. He did this by virtue of his
personal qualities, entirely against the will of the people of England, who, as far as they were politically conscious at all, would
have greatly preferred Harold. But William had all the qualities
that make an individual irresistible: the physical strength and
ferocity of a king of beasts, the political genius of a king of men,
the strategic cunning and tactical gumption of a military genius;
and nothing that France or England could say or do prevailed
against him. What are we to do with such people?

When an established political routine breaks down and produces political chaos, a combination of personal ambition with
military genius and political capacity in a single individual gives
that individual his opportunity. Napoleon, if he had been born
a century earlier, would have had no more chance of becoming
emperor of the French than Marshal Saxe had of supplanting
Louis XV. In spite of the French Revolution, he was a very
ordinary snob in his eighteenth-century social outlook. His assumption of the imperial diadem, his ridiculous attempt to establish the little Buonaparte family on all the thrones under his
control, his remanufacture of a titular aristocracy to make a court
for himself, his silly insistence on imperial etiquette when he was
a dethroned and moribund prisoner in St Helena, shew that, for
all his genius, he was and always had been behind the times. But
he was for a time irresistible because, though he could fight
battles on academic lines only, and was on that point a routineer
soldier, he could play the war game on the established procedure
so superbly that all the armies of Europe crumpled up before him.
It was easy for anti-Bonapartist writers, from Taine to Mr H. G.
Wells, to disparage him as a mere cad; but Goethe, who could
face facts, and on occasion rub them in, said simply "You shake
your chains in vain." Unfortunately for himself and Europe Napoleon was fundamentally a commonplace human fool. In spite of

his early failure in the east he made a frightful draft on the manhood of France for his march to Moscow, only to hurry back leaving his legions dead in the snow, and thereafter go from disaster to disaster. Bernadotte, the lawyer's son who enlisted as a common soldier and ended unconquered on the throne of Sweden (his descendants still hold it), made a far better job of his affairs. When for the first time Napoleon came up against a really original commander at Waterloo, he still made all the textbook moves he had learnt at the military academy, and did not know when he was beaten until it was too late to do anything but run away. Instead of making for America at all hazards he threw himself on the magnanimity of the Prince Regent, who obviously could not have spared him even if he had wanted to. His attempt to wedge himself and his upstart family into the old dynasties by his divorce and his Austrian marriage ended in making him a notorious cuckold. But the vulgarer fool and the paltrier snob you prove Napoleon to have been, the more alarming becomes the fact that this shabby-genteel Corsican subaltern (and a very unsatisfactory subaltern at that) dominated Europe for years, and placed on his own head the crown of Charlemagne. Is there really nothing to be done with such men but submit to them until, having risen by their specialities, they ruin themselves by their vulgarities?

It was easy for Napoleon to make a better job of restoring order after the French Revolution than Sieyès, who tried to do it by writing paper constitutions, or than a plucky bully like Barras, who cared for nothing except feathering his own nest. Any tidy and public spirited person could have done as much with the necessary prestige. Napoleon got that prestige by feeding the popular appetite for military glory. He could not create that natural appetite; but he could feed it by victories; and he could use all the devices of journalism and pageantry and patriotic braggadocio to make La Gloire glorious. And all this because, like William the Conqueror, he had the group of talents that make a successful general and democratic ruler. Had not the French Revolution so completely failed to produce a tolerable government to replace the monarchy it overthrew, and thereby reduced itself to desperation, Napoleon would have been only a famous general like Saxe or Wellington or Marlborough, who under similar circumstances could and indeed must have become kings if they had been ungovernable enough to desire it. Only the other day a man without any of the social advantages of these commanders made himself Shah of Iran.

Julius Cæsar and Cromwell also mounted on the débris of collapsing political systems; and both of them refused crowns. But no crown could have added to the power their military capacity gave them. Cæsar bribed enormously; but there were richer men than he in Rome to play that game. Only, they could not have won the battle of Pharsalia. Cromwell proved invincible in the field—such as it was.

It is not, however, these much hackneyed historical figures that trouble us now. Pharsalias and Dunbars and Waterloos are things of the past: battles nowadays last several months and then peter out on barbed wire under the fire of machine guns. Suppose Ludendorff had been a Napoleon, and Haig a Marlborough, Wellington, and Cromwell rolled into one, what more could they have done than either declare modern war impossible or else keep throwing masses of infantry in the old fashion against slaughtering machinery like pigs in Chicago? Napoleon's booklearnt tactics and the columns that won so many battles for him would have no more chance nowadays than the ragged Irish pikemen on Vinegar Hill; and Wellington's thin red line and his squares would have vanished in the fumes of T.N.T. on the Somme. "The Nelson touch" landed a section of the British fleet at the bottom of the Dardanelles. And yet this war, which, if it did not end civilized war (perhaps it did, by the way, though the War Office may not yet have realized it) at least made an end of the supremacy of the glory virtuoso who can play brilliant variations on the battle of Hastings, has been followed by such a group of upstart autocrats as the world had ceased to suppose possible. Mussolini, Hitler, Kemal and Riza Khan began in the ranks, and have no Marengos to their credit; yet there they are at the top!

Here again the circumstances gave the men their opportunity. Neither Mussolini nor Hitler could have achieved their present personal supremacy when I was born in the middle of the nineteenth century, because the prevailing mentality of that deluded time was still hopefully parliamentary. Democracy was a dream, an ideal. Everything would be well when all men had votes. Everything would be better than well when all women had votes. There was a great fear of public opinion because it was a dumb phantom which every statesman could identify with his own conscience and dread as the Nemesis of unscrupulous ambition. That was the golden age of democracy: the phantom was a real and beneficent force. Many delusions are. In those days even our Conservative rulers agreed that we were a liberty loving people: that, for instance, Englishmen would never tolerate compulsory military service as the slaves of foreign despots did.

It was part of the democratic dream that Parliament was an instrument for carrying out the wishes of the voters, absurdly called its constituents. And as, in the nineteenth century, it was still believed that British individual liberty forbad Parliament to do anything that it could possibly leave to private enterprise, Parliament was able to keep up its reputation by simply maintaining an effective police force and enforcing private contracts. Even Factory Acts and laws against adulteration and sweating were jealously resisted as interferences with the liberty of free Britons. If there was anything wrong, the remedy was an extension of the franchise. Like Hamlet, we lived on the chameleon's dish "air, promise crammed."

But you cannot create a mentality out of promises without having to face occasional demands for their materialization. The Treasury Bench was up for auction at every election, the bidding being in promises. The political parties, finding it much less troublesome to give the people votes than to carry out reforms, at last established adult suffrage.

The result was a colossal disappointment and disillusion. The phantom of Democracy, *alias* Public Opinion, which, acting as an artificial political conscience, had restrained Gladstone and

Disraeli, vanished. The later parliamentary leaders soon learnt from experience that they might with perfect impunity tell the nation one thing on Tuesday and the opposite on Friday without anyone noticing the discrepancy. The donkey had overtaken the carrots at last; and instead of eating them he allowed them to be snatched away from him by any confidence trickster who told him to look up into the sky.

The diplomatists immediately indulged themselves with a prodigiously expensive war, after which the capitalist system, which had undertaken to find employment for everybody at subsistence wages, and which, though it had never fulfilled that undertaking, had at least found employment for enough of them to leave the rest too few to be dangerous, defaulted in respect of unprecedented millions of unemployed, who had to be bought off by doles administered with a meanness and cruelty which revived all the infamies of the Poor Law of a century ago (the days of Oliver Twist) and could not be administered in any kinder way without weakening the willingness of its recipients to prefer even the poorliest paid job to its humiliations.

The only way of escape was for the Government to organize the labor of the unemployed for the supply of their own needs. But Parliament not only could not do this, but could and did prevent its being done. In vain did the voters use their votes to place a Labor Government, with a Cabinet of Socialists, on the Treasury Bench. Parliament took these men, who had been intransigent Socialists and revolutionists all their lives, and reduced them to a condition of political helplessness in which they were indistinguishable except by name from the most re-actionary members of the House of Lords or the military clubs. A Socialist Prime Minister, after trying for years to get the parliamentary car into gear for a move forward, and finding that though it would work easily and smoothly in neutral the only gear that would engage was the reverse gear (popularly called "the axe" because it could do nothing but cut down wages), first formed what he called a national government by a coalition of all parties, and then, having proved by this experiment that it did not make the smallest difference whether members of the Cabinet were the reddest of Bolsheviks or the bluest of Tories, made things easier by handing over his premiership to a colleague who, being a Conservative, and popular and amiable into the bargain, could steal a horse where a Socialist dare not look over a hedge. The voters rejected him at the next election; but he retained his membership of the Cabinet precisely as if he had been triumphantly returned. Bismarck could have done no more.

These events, helped by the terrific moral shock of the war, and the subsequent exposure of the patriotic lying by which the workers of Europe had been provoked to slaughter one another, made an end of the nineteenth century democratic mentality. Parliament fell into contempt; ballot papers were less esteemed than toilet papers; the men from the trenches had no patience with the liberties that had not saved them from being driven like sheep to the shambles.

Of this change our parliamentarians and journalists had no suspicion. Creatures of habit, they went on as if nothing had occurred since Queen Victoria's death except a couple of extensions of the franchise and an epochmaking revolution in Russia which they poohpoohed as a transient outburst of hooliganism fomented by a few bloodthirsty scoundrels, exactly as the American revolution and the French revolution had been poohpoohed when they, too, were contemporary.

Here was clearly a big opportunity for a man psychologist enough to grasp the situation and bold enough to act on it. Such a man was Mussolini. He had become known as a journalist by championing the demobilized soldiers, who, after suffering all the horrors of the war, had returned to find that the men who had been kept at home in the factories comfortably earning good wages, had seized those factories according to the Syndicalist doctrine of "workers' control", and were wrecking them in their helpless ignorance of business. As one indignant master-Fascist said to me "They were listening to speeches round red flags and leaving the cows unmilked."

The demobilized fell on the Syndicalists with sticks and stones.

Some, more merciful, only dosed them with castor oil. They carried Mussolini to Rome with a rush. This gave him the chance of making an irreparable mistake and spending the next fifteen years in prison. It seemed just the occasion for a grand appeal for liberty, for democracy, for a parliament in which the people were supreme: in short, for nineteenth century resurrection pie. Mussolini did not make that mistake. With inspired precision he denounced Liberty as a putrefying corpse. He declared that what people needed was not liberty but discipline, the sterner the better. He said that he would not tolerate Oppositions: he called for action and silence. The people, instead of being shocked like good Liberals, rose to him. He was able to organize a special constabulary who wore black shirts and applied the necessary coercion.

Such improvised bodies attracted young men of military tastes and old soldiers, inevitably including a percentage of ruffians and Sadists. This fringe of undesirables soon committed outrages and a couple of murders, whereupon all the Liberal newspapers in Europe shrieked with horror as if nothing else was happening in Italy. Mussolini refused to be turned aside from his work like a parliamentary man to discuss "incidents." All he said was "I take the responsibility for everything that has happened." When the Italian Liberals joined in the shrieking he seized the shriekers and transported them to the Lipari Isles. Parliament, openly flouted, chastised, and humiliated, could do nothing. The people were delighted; for that was just how they wanted to see Parliament treated. The doctrinaires of liberty fled to France and England, preferring them to Lipari, and wrote eloquent letters to the papers demanding whether every vestige of freedom, freedom of speech, freedom of the press, freedom of Parliament, was to be trampled under the heel of a ruthless dictator merely because the Italian trains were running punctually and travellers in Italy could depend on their luggage not being stolen without actually sitting on it. The English editors gave them plenty of space, and wrote sympathetic articles paraphrasing John Stuart Mill's Essay on Liberty. Mussolini, now Il Duce, never even looked round:

he was busy sweeping up the elected municipalities, and replacing them with efficient commissioners of his own choice, who had to do their job or get out. The editors had finally to accord him a sort of Pragmatic Sanction by an admission that his plan worked better than the old plan; but they were still blind to the fact staring them in the face that Il Duce, knowing what the people wanted and giving it to them, was responding to the real democratic urge whilst the cold tealeaves of the nineteenth century were making them sick. It was evident that Mussolini was master of Italy as far as such mastership is possible; but what was not evident to English-men who had had their necks twisted the other way from their childhood was that even when he deliberately spat in the face of the League of Nations at Corfu, and defiantly asked the Powers whether they had anything to say about it, he was delighting his own people by the spectacle of a great Italian bullying the world, and getting away with it triumphantly. Parliaments are supposed to have their fingers always on the people's pulse and to respond to its slightest throb. Mussolini proved that parliaments have not the slightest notion of how the people are feeling, and that he, being a good psychologist and a man of the people himself to boot, was a true organ of democracy.

I, being a bit of a psychologist myself, also understood the situation, and was immediately denounced by the refugees and their champions as an anti-democrat, a hero worshipper of tyrants, and all the rest of it.

Hitler's case was different; but he had one quality in common with Il Duce: he knew what the victorious Allies would fight for and what they would only bluster about. They had already been forced to recognize that their demands for plunder had gone far beyond Germany's utmost resources. But there remained the clauses of the Versailles treaty by which Germany was to be kept in a condition of permanent, decisive, and humiliating mili-tary inferiority to the other Powers, and especially to France. Hitler was political psychologist enough to know that the time had arrived when it would be quite impossible for the Allies to begin the war over again to enforce these clauses. He saw his opportunity and took it. He violated the clauses, and declared that he was going to go on violating them until a fully re-armed Germany was on equal terms with the victors. He did not soften his defiance by any word of argument or diplomacy. He knew that his attitude was safe and sure of success; and he took care to make it as defiant as that of Ajax challenging the lightning. The Powers had either to renew the war or tear up the impossible clauses with a good grace. But they could not grasp the situation, and went on nagging pitifully about the wickedness of breaking a treaty. Hilter said that if they mentioned that subject again Germany would withdraw from the League of Nations and cut the Powers dead. He bullied and snubbed as the man who understands a situation can always bully and snub the nincompoops who are only whining about it. He at once became a popular idol, and had the regular executive forces so completely devoted to him that he was able to disband the brownshirted constabulary he had organized on the Mussolini model. He met the conventional democratic challenge by plebiscites of ninety per cent in his favor. The myopia of the Powers had put him in a position so far stronger than Mussolini's that he was able to kill seventy-seven of his most dangerous opponents at a blow and then justify himself completely before an assembly fully as representative as the British Parliament, the climax being his appointment as absolute dictator in Germany for life, a stretch of Cæsarism no nineteenth century Hohenzollern would have dreamt of demanding.

Hitler was able to go further than Mussolini because he had a defeated, plundered, humiliated nation to rescue and restore, whereas Mussolini had only an irritated but victorious one. He carried out a persecution of the Jews which went to the scandalous length of outlawing, plundering, and exiling Albert Einstein, a much greater man than any politician, but great in such a manner that he was quite above the heads of the masses and therefore so utterly powerless economically and militarily that he depended for his very existence on the culture and conscience of the rulers of the earth. Hitler's throwing Einstein

to the Antisemite wolves was an appalling breach of cultural
faith. It raised the question which is the root question of this
preface: to wit, what safeguard have the weaponless great against
the great who have myrmidons at their call? It is the most
frightful betrayal of civilization for the rulers who monopolize
physical force to withhold their protection from the pioneers in
thought. Granted that they are sometimes forced to do it because intellectual advances may present themselves as quackery,
sedition, obscenity, or blasphemy, and always present themselves as heresies. Had Einstein been formally prosecuted and
sentenced by the German National Socialist State, as Galileo was
prosecuted by the Church, for shaking the whole framework
of established physical science by denying the infallibility of
Newton, introducing fantastic factors into mathematics, destroying human faith in absolute measurement, and playing an incomprehensible trick with the sacred velocity of light, quite a
strong case could have been made out by the public prosecutor.
But to set the police on him because he was a Jew could be
justified only on the ground that the Jews are the natural enemies
of the rest of the human race, and that as a state of perpetual war
necessarily exists between them any Gentile has the same reason
for killing any Jew at sight as the Roman soldier had for killing
Archimedes.

Now no doubt Jews are most obnoxious creatures. Any com-
petent historian or psycho-analyst can bring a mass of incon-
trovertible evidence to prove that it would have been better for
the world if the Jews had never existed. But I, as an Irishman,
can, with patriotic relish, demonstrate the same of the English.
Also of the Irish. If Herr Hitler would only consult the French
and British newspapers and magazines of the latter half of 1914,
he would learn that the Germans are a race of savage idolaters,
murderers, liars, and fiends whose assumption of the human form
is thinner than that of the wolf in Little Red Riding Hood.

We all live in glass houses. Is it wise to throw stones at the
Jews? Is it wise to throw stones at all?

Herr Hitler is not only an Antisemite, but a believer in the possibility and desirability of a pure bred German race. I should like to ask him why. All Germans are not Mozarts, nor even Mendelssohns and Meyerbeers, both of whom, by the way, though exceptionally desirable Germans, were Jews. Surely the average German can be improved. I am told that children bred from Irish colleens and Chinese laundrymen are far superior to inbred Irish or Chinese. Herr Hitler is not a typical German. I should not be at all surprised if it were discovered that his very mixed blood (all our bloods today are hopelessly mixed) got fortified somewhere in the past by that of King David. He cannot get over the fact that the lost tribes of Israel expose us all to the suspicion (sometimes, as in Abyssinia, to the boast) that we are those lost tribes, or at least that we must have absorbed them.

One of my guesses in this matter is that Herr Hitler in his youth was fascinated by Houston Chamberlain's Foundations of the XIX Century, an interesting book which at the time of its appearance I recommended everybody to read. Its ethnology was not wholly imaginary. A smattering of Mendelism is all that one needs to know that the eternal fusion of races does not always blend them. The Jews will often throw up an apparently pure-bred Hittite or a pure-bred Philistine. The Germans throw up out-and-out blond beasts side by side with dark Saturnine types like the Führer himself. I am a blond, much less an antique Roman than a Dane. One of my sisters was a brunette: the other had hair of a flaming red seen only in the Scottish Highlands, to which my ancestry has been traced. All these types with which writers like Chamberlain play: the Teutons and Latins, the Apollonians and Dionysians, the Nordics and Southics, the Dominants and Recessives, have existed and keep cropping up as individuals, and exciting antipathies or affinities quite often enough to give substance to theories about them; but the notion that they can be segregated as races or species is bosh. We have nations with national characteristics (rapidly fading, by the way), national languages, and national customs. But they deteriorate without cross fertilization; and if Herr Hitler could put a stop to cross fertilization in Germany and produce a population of brainless

Bismarcks Germany would be subjugated by crossfertilized aliens, possibly by cosmopolitan Jews. There is more difference between a Catholic Bavarian and a Lutheran Prussian, between a tall fair Saxon and a stocky Baltic Celt, than there is between a Frankfort Jew and a Frankfort Gentile. Even in Africa, where pink emigrants struggle with brown and black natives for possession of the land, and our Jamaican miscegenation shocks public sentiment, the sun sterilizes the pinks to such an extent that Cabinet ministers call for more emigration to maintain the pink population. They do not yet venture to suggest that the pinks had better darken their skins with a mixture of Bantu or Zulu blood; but that conclusion is obvious. In New Zealand, in Hawaii, there are pure-bred pinks and yellows; but there are hardly any pure-bred Maories or South Sea Islanders left. In Africa the intelligent pink native is a Fusionist as between Dutch and British stock. The intelligent Jew is a Fusionist as between Jew and Gentile stock, even when he is also a bit of a Zionist. Only the stupidest or craziest ultra-Nationalists believe that people corralled within the same political frontier are all exactly alike, and that they improve by continuous inbreeding.

Now Herr Hitler is not a stupid German. I therefore urge upon him that his Antisemitism and national exclusiveness must be pathological: a craze, a complex, a bee in his bonnet, a hole in his armor, a hitch in his statesmanship, one of those lesions which sometimes prove fatal. As it has no logical connection with Fascism or National Socialism, and has no effect on them except to bring them into disrepute, I doubt whether it can survive its momentary usefulness as an excuse for plundering raids and *coups d'état* against inconvenient Liberals or Marxists. A persecution is always a man hunt; and man hunting is not only a very horrible sport but socially a dangerous one, as it revives a primitive instinct incompatible with civilization: indeed civilization rests fundamentally on the compact that it shall be dropped.

And here comes the risk we run when we allow a dominant individual to become a despot. There is a story told of a pious man who was sustained through a lifetime of crushing misfortune by his steady belief that if he fought the good fight to the end he would at last stand in the presence of his God. In due course he died, and presented himself at the gates of heaven for his reward. St Peter, who was for some reason much worried, hastily admitted him and bade him go and enjoy himself. But the good man said that he did not want to enjoy himself: he wanted to stand in the presence of God. St Peter tried to evade the claim, dwelling on the other delights of heaven, coaxing, bullying, arguing. All in vain: he could not shake the claimant and could not deny his right. He sent for St Paul, who was as worried and as evasive as his colleague; but he also failed to induce the newcomer to forgo his promised privilege. At last they took him by the arms and led him to a mighty cathedral, where, entering by the west door, he saw the Ancient of Days seated in silent majesty on a throne in the choir. He sprang forward to prostrate himself at the divine feet, but was held back firmly by the apostles. "Be quiet" said St Paul. "He has gone mad; and we dont know what to do." "Dont tell anybody" added St Peter. And there the story ends.

But that is not how the story ends on earth. Make any common fellow an autocrat and at once you have the Beggar on Horseback riding to the devil. Even when, as the son of his father, he has been trained from infancy to behave well in harness and blinkers, he may go as mad sadistically as a Roman emperor or a Russian Tsar. But that is only the extreme case. Uncommon people, promoted on their merits, are by no means wholly exempt from megalomania. Morris's simple and profound saying that "no man is good enough to be another man's master" holds good unless both master and man regard themselves as equally the fellow servants of God in States where God still reigns, or, in States where God is dead, as the subjects and agents of a political constitution applying humane principles which neither of them may violate. In that case autocrats are no longer autocrats. Failing any such religious or political creed all autocrats go more or less mad. That is a plain fact of political pathology.

Judged in this light our present predicament is lamentable. We no longer believe in the old "sanctions" (as they are called nowadays) of heaven and hell; and except in Russia there is not in force a single political constitution that enables and enjoins the citizen to earn his own living as a matter of elementary honesty, or that does not exalt vast personal riches and the organization of slaughter and conquest above all other conditions and activities. The financier and the soldier are the cocks of the walk; and democracy means that their parasites and worshippers carry all before them.

Thus when so many other tyrannies have been swept away by simple Liberalism, the tyranny of the talented individuals will remain. Again I ask what are we to do with them in self-defence? Mere liquidation would be disastrous, because at present only about five per cent of the population are capable of making decisions of any importance; and without many daily decisions civilization would go to pieces. The problem is how to make sure that the decisions shall be made in the general interest and not solely in the immediate personal interest of the decider. It was argued by our classical political economists that there is a divine harmony between these two interests of such a nature that if every decider does the best for himself the result will also be the best for everybody. In spite of a century of bitter experience of the adoption of these excuses for laziness in politics, shameless selfishness in industry, and glorification of idle uselessness in the face of the degrading misery of the masses, they are still taught in our universities, and, what is worse, broadcast by university professors by wireless, as authentic political economy instead of what they really are: that is, the special pleading put forward in defence of the speculators, exploiters, and parasitic property owners in whose grossly antisocial interests the country is misgoverned. Since Karl Marx and Friedrich Engels exposed the horrible condition of the working classes that underlies the pursepride and snobbery of the upper middle classes and the prestige of the landed gentry and peerage there has been no substantial excuse for believing in the alleged harmony of interests. Nothing more diabolical can be conceived than the destiny of a civilization in which the material sources

123

of the people's subsistence are privately owned by a handful of persons taught from childhood that every penny they can extort from the propertyless is an addition to the prosperity of their country and an enrichment of the world at large.

But private property is not the subject of my demonstration in The Millionairess. Private property can be communized. Capitalists and landlords can be pressed into the service of the community, or, if they are idle or incorrigibly recalcitrant, handed over to the police. Under such circumstances the speculator would find his occupation gone. With him would disappear the routine exploiter. But the decider, the dominator, the organizer, the tactician, the mesmerizer would remain; and if they were still educated as ladies and gentlemen are educated today, and consequently had the same sort of consciences and ambitions, they would, if they had anything like our present proletariat to deal with, re-establish industrial anarchy and heritable private property in land with all their disastrous consequences and Gadarene destiny. And their rule, being that of able persons and not of nincompoops born with silver spoons in their mouths, would at first produce some striking improvements in the working of the public services, including the elimination of dud dignitaries and the general bracing up of plodders and slackers. But when dominators die, and are succeeded by persons who can only work a routine, a relapse is inevitable; and the destruction by the dominators of the organizations by which citizens defend themselves against oppression (trade unions, for example) may be found to leave society less organized than it was before the hand of the master had risen from the dust to which it has returned. For it is obvious that a business organized for control by an exceptionally omnipotent and omniscient head will go to pieces when that head is replaced by a commonplace numskull. We need not go back to Richard Cromwell or the Duke of Reichstadt to illustrate this. It is occurring every day in commercial business.

Now the remedy lies, not in the extermination of all dominators and deciders, but on the contrary in their multiplication to what may be called their natural minority limit, which will destroy their present scarcity value. But we must also eliminate the mass of ignorance, weakness, and timidity which force them to treat fools according to their folly. Armies, fanatical sects and mobs, and the blackshirts complained of today by their black and blue victims, have consisted hitherto mostly of people who should not exist in civilized society. Titus Oates and Lord George Gordon owed their vogue to the London mob. There should not have been any London mob. The soldiers of Marlborough and Wellington were never-do-wells, mental defectives, and laborers with the minds and habits of serfs. Military geniuses could hunt with such products more easily than with a pack of hounds. Our public school and university education equips armies of this kind with appropriate staffs of officers. When both are extinct we shall be able to breathe more freely.

Let us therefore assume that the soldier and his officer as we know them, the Orange and Papist rioters of Belfast, the Moslem and Hindu irreconcilables of the east and the Ku-Klux-Klans and lynching mobs of the west, have passed away as the less dangerous prehistoric monsters have passed, and that all men and women are meeting on equal terms as far as circumstances and education are concerned. Let us suppose that no man can starve or flog his fellows into obeying him, or force upon them the alternative of risking their lives for him in battle or being shot at dawn. Let us take for granted armies intelligent enough to present their officers at any moment with the alternative of organizing a return home or being superseded out of hand. Let us narrow the case to the mysterious precedence into which certain people get pushed even when they lack ambition and are far too intelligent to believe that eminence and its responsibilities are luxuries. To be "greatest among you" is a distinction dearly bought at the price of being "servant to all the rest." Plato was quite right in taking reluctance to govern as a leading symptom of supreme fitness for it. But if we insisted on this qualification in all cases, we should find ourselves as short of governors as the churches would be if they insisted on all their parish priests or rectors being saints. A great deal of the directing and

organizing work of the world will still have to be done by energetic and capable careerists who are by no means void of vulgar
ambition, and very little troubled by the responsibilities that
attend on power. When I said that Napoleon was fundamentally
a fool and a snob I did not mean for a moment to question his
extraordinary capacity as a ruler of men. If we compare him with
his valet-secretary Bourrienne we find that there were no external
circumstances to prevent Bourrienne becoming the emperor and
Napoleon the valet. They quarrelled and parted with an exchange
of epithets unprintable in polite English. Bourrienne was as much
a Man of Destiny as Buonaparte. But it was his destiny to be ruled
and Buonaparte's to rule; and so Buonaparte became Napoleon
Bonaparte, First Consul and Emperor, as inevitably as Bourrienne
remained a speculator, litterateur and diplomatist. I am not for-
getting that Bourrienne saw Napoleon come and go, and had a
much more comfortable and finally a more successful career than
his quondam master; but the point is that Napoleon was master
whilst their personal relations lasted. And please note that Napoleon did not and could not impose on Bourrienne and Talleyrand,
nor even on the more cultivated of his marshals (all planetary
Napoleons) as he could and did on the soldiery and peasantry.
They turned against him very promptly when his fortunes
changed and he could no longer be of any use to them.

Now if a ruler can command men only as long as he is efficient
and successful his rule is neither a tyranny nor a calamity: it is a
very valuable asset. But suppose the nation is made up for the
most part of people too ignorant to understand efficient government, and taught, as far as they are taught at all, to measure
greatness by pageantry and the wholesale slaughter called military
glory. It was this ignorance and idolatry that first exalted
Napoleon and then smashed him. From Toulon to Austerlitz
Napoleon did what good he did by stealth, and had no occasion
to "blush to find it fame," as nobody gave him the least credit for
anything but killing. When the glory turned to shame on the road
back from Moscow his good works availed him nothing, and the
way was open to St Helena. Catherine of Russia, when she was

faced with a revolt against the misery of her people, said, not "Let us relieve their misery by appropriate reforms," but " Let us give them a little war to amuse them." Every tottering regime tries to rally its subjects to its support in the last resort by a war. It was not only the last card of Napoleon III before he lost the game: it played a considerable part in the capitalist support of Hohenzollern sabre rattling which made the desperate onslaught of Germany in 1914 possible. Patriotism, roused to boiling point by an enemy at the gate, is not only the last refuge of a scoundrel in Dr. Johnson's sense, it is far more dangerously the everyday resort of capitalism and feudalism as a red herring across the scent of Communism. Under such circumstances it is fortunate that war on the modern scale is so completely beyond the capacity of private capitalism that, as in 1915, it forces the belligerents into national factory production, public discipline, and rationed distribution: in short, into Socialism. Not only did national factories spring up like mushrooms, but the private factories had to be brought up to the mark by public control of prices and dictation of scientific business methods, involving such an exposure of the obsolescence and inefficiency of profitmongering methods that it took years of reckless lying from Press and platform to make the silly public believe the contrary. For war is like the seven magic bullets which the devil has ready to sell for a human soul. Six of them may hit the glorymonger's mark very triumphantly; but the seventh plays some unexpected and unintended trick that upsets the gunman's apple cart. It seemed an astute stroke of German imperial tactics to send Lenin safely through Germany to Russia so that he might make trouble for the Tsar. But the bullet was a number seven: it killed the Tsar very efficiently; but it came back like a boomerang and laid the Hohenzollerns beside the Romanoffs.

Pageantry will lose its black magic when it becomes a local popular amusement; so that the countryside may come to know it from behind the scenes, when, though it will still please, it will no longer impose. For mere iconoclasm is a mistake: the Roundhead folly (really a Thickhead one) of destroying the power of

127

the pageant by forbidding all theatrical displays and dressings-up, and making everybody wear ugly clothes, ended in the flamboyant profligacy of the Restoration; and the attempt to enforce the second commandment by smashing the images soon smashed the second commandment. Give away the secret that the dressed-up performers are only amateurs, and the images works of art, and the dupes and worshippers will become undeluded connoisseurs.

Unfortunately it is easier to produce a nation of artistic than of political connoisseurs. Our schools and universities do not concern themselves with fine art, which they despise as an unmanly pursuit. It is possible for a young gentleman to go through the whole educational mill of preparatory school, public school, and university with the highest academic honors without knowing the difference between a chanty and a symphony, a tavern sign and a portrait by Titian, a ballad by Macaulay and a stanza by Keats. But at least he is free to find out all this for himself if he has a fancy that way.

Not so in political science. Not so in religion. In these subjects he is proselytized from the beginning in the interests of established institutions so effectually that he remains all his life firmly convinced that his greatest contemporaries are rascally and venal agitators, villainous blasphemers, or at best seditious cads. He will listen to noodles' orations, read pompous leading articles, and worship the bloodthirsty tribal idols of Noah and Samuel with a gravity and sincerity that would make him infinitely pitiable if they did not also make him infinitely dangerous. He will feed his mind on empty phrases as Nebuchadnezzar fed his body on grass; and any boss who has mastered these phrases can become his dictator, his despot, his evangelist, and in effect his god-emperor.

Clearly we shall be bossridden in one form or another as long as education means being put through this process, or the best imitation of it that our children's parents can afford. The remedy is another Reformation, now long and perilously overdue, in the direction and instruction of our children's minds politically and religiously. We should begin well to the left of Russia, which is still encumbered with nineteenth century superstitions. Communism is the fairy godmother who can transform Bosses into "servants to all the rest"; but only a creed of Creative Evolution can set the souls of the people free. Then the dominator will still find himself face to face with subordinates who can do nothing without him; but that will not give him the inside grip. A late rich shipowner, engaged in a quarrel with his workmen in which he assumed that I was on their side, rashly asked me what his men could do without him. Naturally I asked him what he could do without them, hoping to open his eyes to the fact that apart from the property rights he had bought or borrowed he was as dependent on them as they on him. But I fear I impressed him most by adding, quite untruly, that no gentleman would have asked that question.

Save for my allusion to the persecution and exile of Einstein I have not said a word here about the miserable plight of the great men neglected, insulted, starved, and occasionally put to death, sometimes horribly, by the little ones. Their case is helpless because nothing can defend them against the might of overwhelming numbers unless and until they develop the Vril imagined by Bulwer-Lytton which will enable one person to destroy a multitude, and thereby make us more particular than we are at present about the sort of persons we produce. I am confining myself to the power wielded by the moneymakers and military geniuses in political life and by the dominant personalities in private life. Lytton's Vril was a fiction only in respect of its being available for everybody, and therefore an infallible preventive of any attempt at oppression. For that individuals here and there possess a power of domination which others are unable to resist is undeniable; and since this power is as yet nameless we may as well call it Vril as anything else. It is the final reality of inequality. It is easy to equalize the dominators with the commonplacers economically: you just give one of them half-a-crown and the other two-and-sixpence. Nelson was paid no more than any other naval captain or admiral; and the poverty of Mozart or Marx was worse than the voluntary holy poverty of the great heads of the religious orders. Dominators and dominated are already equalized before the law: shall not I, a playwright of Shakesperean eminence, be hanged if I commit a murder precisely as if I were the most illiterate call boy? Politically we all have at least the symbol of equality in our votes, useless as they are to us under political and economic institutions made to encourage William the Conqueror to slay Harold and exploit Hodge. But, I repeat, when all these perfectly feasible equalizations are made real, there still remains Epifania, shorn of her millions and unable to replace them, but still as dominant as Saint Joan, Saint Clare, and Saint Teresa. The most complete Communism and Democracy can only give her her chance far more effectively than any feudal or capitalist society.

And this, I take it, is one of the highest claims of Communism and Democracy to our consideration, and the explanation of the apparently paradoxical fact that it is always the greatest spirits, from Jesus to Lenin, from St Thomas More to William Morris, who are communists and democrats, and always the commonplace people who weary us with their blitherings about the impossibility of equality when they are at a loss for any better excuse for keeping other people in the kitchen and themselves in the drawing room. I say cheerfully to the dominators "By all means dominate: it is up to us to so order our institutions that you shall not oppress us, nor bequeath any of your precedence to your commonplace children." For when ambition and greed and mere brainless energy have been disabled, the way will be clear for inspiration and aspiration to save us from the fatheaded stagnation of the accursed Victorian snobbery which is bringing us to the verge of ruin.

MALVERN,
   28th August 1935.

THE MILLIONAIRESS

ACT I

Mr Julius Sagamore, a smart young solicitor, is in his office in Lincoln's Inn Fields. It is a fine morning in May. The room, an old panelled one, is so arranged that Mr Sagamore, whom we see sitting under the window in profile with his back to it and his left side presented to us, is fenced off by his writing table from excessive intimacy with emotional clients or possible assault by violent or insane ones. The door is on his right towards the farther end of the room. The faces of the clients are thus illuminated by the window whilst his own countenance is in shadow. The fireplace, of Adams design, is in the wall facing him. It is surmounted by a dingy portrait of a judge. In the wall on his right, near the corner farthest from him, is the door, with a cleft pediment enshrining a bust of some other judge. The rest of this wall is occupied by shelves of calf-bound law books. The wall behind Mr Sagamore has the big window as aforesaid, and beside it a stand of black tin boxes inscribed with clients' names.

So far, the place proclaims the eighteenth century; but as the year is 1935, *and Mr Sagamore has no taste for dust and mould, and requires a room which suggests opulence, and in which lady clients will look their best, everything is well dusted and polished; the green carpet is new, rich, and thick; and the half dozen chairs, four of which are ranged under the bookshelves, are Chippendales of the very latest fake. Of the other two one is occupied by himself, and the other stands half way between his table and the fireplace for the accommodation of his clients.*

The telephone, on the table at his elbow, rings.

SAGAMORE [*listening*] Yes? . . . [*Impressed*] Oh! Send her up at once.

A tragic looking woman, athletically built and expensively dressed, storms into the room. He rises obsequiously.

THE LADY. Are you Julius Sagamore, the worthless nephew of my late solicitor Pontifex Sagamore?

SAGAMORE. I do not advertize myself as worthless; but Pontifex Sagamore was my uncle; and I have returned from Australia to succeed to as much of his business as I can persuade his clients to trust me with.

THE LADY. I have heard him speak of you; and I naturally concluded that as you had been packed off to Australia you must be worthless. But it does not matter, as my business is very simple. I desire to make my will, leaving everything I possess to my husband. You can hardly go wrong about that, I suppose.

SAGAMORE. I shall do my best. Pray sit down.

THE LADY. No: I am restless. I shall sit down when I feel tired.

SAGAMORE. As you please. Before I draw up the will it will be necessary for me to know who your husband is.

THE LADY. My husband is a fool and a blackguard. You will state that fact in the will. You will add that it was his conduct that drove me to commit suicide.

SAGAMORE. But you have not committed suicide.

THE LADY. I shall have, when the will is signed.

SAGAMORE. Of course, quite so: stupid of me. And his name?

THE LADY. His name is Alastair Fitzfassenden.

SAGAMORE. What! The amateur tennis champion and heavy weight boxer?

THE LADY. Do you know him?

SAGAMORE. Every morning we swim together at the club.

THE LADY. The acquaintance does you little credit.

SAGAMORE. I had better tell you that he and I are great friends, Mrs Fitzfassen—

THE LADY. Do not call me by his detestable name. Put me in your books as Epifania Ognisanti di Parerga.

SAGAMORE [bowing] Oh! I am indeed honored. Pray be seated.

EPIFANIA. Sit down yourself; and dont fuss.

SAGAMORE. If you prefer it, certainly. [He sits]. Your father was a very wonderful man, madam.

EPIFANIA. My father was the greatest man in the world. And he died a pauper. I shall never forgive the world for that.

SAGAMORE. A pauper! You amaze me. It was reported that he

THE MILLIONAIRESS

left you, his only child, thirty millions.

EPIFANIA. Well, what was thirty millions to him? He lost a hundred and fifty millions. He had promised to leave me two hundred millions. I was left with a beggarly thirty. It broke his heart.

SAGAMORE. Still, an income of a million and a half—

EPIFANIA. Man: you forget the death duties. I have barely seven hundred thousand a year. Do you know what that means to a woman brought up on an income of seven figures? The humiliation of it!

SAGAMORE. You take away my breath, madam.

EPIFANIA. As I am about to take my own breath away, I have no time to attend to yours.

SAGAMORE. Oh, the suicide! I had forgotten that.

EPIFANIA. Had you indeed? Well, will you please give your mind to it for a moment, and draw up a will for me to sign, leaving everything to Alastair.

SAGAMORE. To humiliate him?

EPIFANIA. No. To ruin him. To destroy him. To make him a beggar on horseback so that he may ride to the devil. Money goes to his head. I have seen it at work on him.

SAGAMORE. I also have seen that happen. But you cannot be sure. He might marry some sensible woman.

EPIFANIA. You are right. Make it a condition of the inheritance that within a month from my funeral he marries a low female named Polly Seedystockings.

SAGAMORE [making a note of it] A funny name.

EPIFANIA. Her real name is Patricia Smith. But her letters to Alastair are signed Polly Seedystockings, as a hint, I suppose, that she wants him to buy her another dozen.

SAGAMORE [taking another sheet of paper and writing] I should like to know Polly.

EPIFANIA. Pray why?

SAGAMORE [talking as he writes] Well, if Alastair prefers her to you she must be indeed worth knowing. I shall certainly make him introduce me.

133

EPIFANIA. You are hardly tactful, Julius Sagamore.

SAGAMORE. That will not matter when you have taken this [*he hands her what he has written*].

EPIFANIA. Whats this?

SAGAMORE. For the suicide. You will have to sign the chemist's book for the cyanide. Say it is for a wasp's nest. The tartaric acid is harmless: the chemist will think you want it to make lemonade. Put the two separately in just enough water to dissolve them. When you mix the two solutions the tartaric and potash will combine and make tartrate of potash. This, being insoluble, will be precipitated to the bottom of the glass; and the supernatant fluid will be pure hydrocyanic acid, one sip of which will kill you like a thunderbolt.

EPIFANIA [*fingering the prescription rather disconcertedly*] You seem to take my death very coolly, Mr Sagamore.

SAGAMORE. I am used to it.

EPIFANIA. Do you mean to tell me that you have so many clients driven to despair that you keep a prescription for them?

SAGAMORE. I do. It's infallible.

EPIFANIA. You are sure that they have all died painlessly and instantaneously?

SAGAMORE. No. They are all alive.

EPIFANIA. Alive! The prescription is a harmless fraud!

SAGAMORE. No. It's a deadly poison. But they dont take it.

EPIFANIA. Why?

SAGAMORE. I dont know. But they never do.

EPIFANIA. I will. And I hope you will be hanged for giving it to me.

SAGAMORE. I am only acting as your solicitor. You say you are going to commit suicide; and you come to me for advice. I do my best for you, so that you can die without wasting a lot of gas or jumping into the Serpentine. Six and eightpence I shall charge your executors.

EPIFANIA. For advising me how to kill myself!

SAGAMORE. Not today. Tomorrow.

EPIFANIA. Why put it off until tomorrow?

THE MILLIONAIRESS

SAGAMORE. Well, it will do as well tomorrow as today. And something amusing may happen this evening. Or even tomorrow evening. Theres no hurry.

EPIFANIA. You are a brute, a beast, and a pig. My life is nothing to you: you do not even ask what has driven me to this. You make money out of the death of your clients.

SAGAMORE. I do. There will be a lot of business connected with your death. Alastair is sure to come to me to settle your affairs.

EPIFANIA. And you expect me to kill myself to make money for you?

SAGAMORE. Well, it is you who have raised my expectations, madam.

EPIFANIA. O God, listen to this man! Has it ever occurred to you that when a woman's life is wrecked she needs a little sympathy and not a bottle of poison?

SAGAMORE. I really cant sympathize with suicide. It doesnt appeal to me, somehow. Still, if it has to be done, it had better be done promptly and scientifically.

EPIFANIA. You dont even ask what Alastair has done to me?

SAGAMORE. It wont matter what he has done to you when you are dead. Why bother about it?

EPIFANIA. You are an unmitigated hog, Julius Sagamore.

SAGAMORE. Why worry about me? The prescription will cure everything.

EPIFANIA. Damn your prescription. There! [*She tears it up and throws the pieces in his face*].

SAGAMORE [*beaming*] It's infallible. And now that you have blown off steam, suppose you sit down and tell me all about it.

EPIFANIA. You call the outcry of an anguished heart blowing off steam, do you?

SAGAMORE. Well, what else would you call it?

EPIFANIA. You are not a man: you are a rhinoceros. You are also a fool.

SAGAMORE. I am only a solicitor.

EPIFANIA. You are a rotten solicitor. You are not a gentleman.

You insult me in my distress. You back up my husband against me. You have no decency, no understanding. You are a fish with the soul of a blackbeetle. Do you hear?

SAGAMORE. Yes: I hear. And I congratulate myself on the number of actions for libel I shall have to defend if you do me the honor of making me your solicitor.

EPIFANIA. You are wrong. I never utter a libel. My father instructed me most carefully in the law of libel. If I questioned your solvency, that would be a libel. If I suggested that you are unfaithful to your wife, that would be a libel. But if I call you a rhinoceros—which you are: a most unmitigated rhinoceros—that is only vulgar abuse. I take good care to confine myself to vulgar abuse; and I have never had an action for libel taken against me. Is that the law, or is it not?

SAGAMORE. I really dont know. I will look it up in my law books.

EPIFANIA. You need not. I instruct you that it is the law. My father always had to instruct his lawyers in the law whenever he did anything except what everybody was doing every day. Solicitors know nothing of law: they are only good at practice, as they call it. My father was a great man: every day of his life he did things that nobody else ever dreamt of doing. I am not, perhaps, a great woman; but I am his daughter; and as such I am an unusual woman. You will take the law from me and do exactly what I tell you to do.

SAGAMORE. That will simplify our relations considerably, madam.

EPIFANIA. And remember this. I have no sense of humor. I will not be laughed at.

SAGAMORE. I should not dream of laughing at a client with an income of three quarters of a million.

EPIFANIA. Have you a sense of humor?

SAGAMORE. I try to keep it in check; but I am afraid I have a little. You appeal to it, somehow.

EPIFANIA. Then I tell you in cold blood, after the most careful consideration of my words, that you are a heartless blackguard.

My distress, my disgrace, my humiliation, the horrible mess and failure I have made of my life seem to you merely funny. If it were not that my father warned me never to employ a solicitor who had no sense of humor I would walk out of this office and deprive you of a client whose business may prove a fortune to you.

SAGAMORE. But, my dear lady, I dont know anything about your distress, your disgrace, the mess you have made of your life and all the rest of it. How can I laugh at things I dont know? If I am laughing—and am I really laughing?—I assure you I am laughing, not at your misfortunes, but at you.

EPIFANIA. Indeed? Am I so comic a figure in my misery?

SAGAMORE. But what is your misery? Do, pray, sit down.

EPIFANIA. You seem to have one idea in your head, and that is to get your clients to sit down. Well, to oblige you. [*She sits down with a flounce. The back of the chair snaps off short with a loud crack. She springs up*]. Oh, I cannot even sit down in a chair without out wrecking it. There is a curse on me.

SAGAMORE [*collapses on the table, shaking with uncontrollable laughter*] ! ! ! ! !

EPIFANIA. Ay: laugh, laugh, laugh. Fool! Clown!

SAGAMORE [*rising resolutely and fetching another chair from the wall*] My best faked Chippendale gone. It cost me four guineas. [*Placing the chair for her*] Now will you please sit down as gently as you can, and stop calling me names? Then, if you wish, you can tell me what on earth is the matter. [*He picks up the broken-off back of the chair and puts it on the table*].

EPIFANIA [*sitting down with dignity*] The breaking of that chair has calmed and relieved me, somehow. I feel as if I had broken your neck, as I wanted to. Now listen to me. [*He comes to her and looks down gravely at her*]. And dont stand over me like that. Sit down on what is left of your sham Chippendale.

SAGAMORE. Certainly [*he sits*]. Now go ahead.

EPIFANIA. My father was the greatest man in the world. I was his only child. His one dread was that I should make a foolish marriage, and lose the little money he was able to leave me.

SAGAMORE. The thirty millions. Precisely.

EPIFANIA. Dont interrupt me. He made me promise that whenever a man asked me to marry him I should impose a condition on my consent.

SAGAMORE [*attentive*] So? What condition?

EPIFANIA. I was to give him one hundred and fifty pounds, and tell him that if within six months he had turned that hundred and fifty pounds into fifty thousand, I was his. If not, I was never to see him again. I saw the wisdom of this. Nobody but my father could have thought of such a real, infallible, unsentimental test. I gave him my sacred promise that I would carry it out faithfully.

SAGAMORE. And you broke that promise. I see.

EPIFANIA. What do you mean—broke that promise?

SAGAMORE. Well, you married Alastair. Now Alastair is a dear good fellow—one of the best in his way—but you are not going to persuade me that he made fifty thousand pounds in six months with a capital of one hundred and fifty.

EPIFANIA. He did. Wise as my father was, he sometimes forgot the wise things he said five minutes after he said them. He warned me that ninety per cent of our selfmade millionaires are criminals who have taken a five hundred to one chance and got away with it by pure luck. Well, Alastair was that sort of criminal.

SAGAMORE. No no: not a criminal. That is not like Alastair. A fool, perhaps, in business. But not a criminal.

EPIFANIA. Like all solicitors you think you know more about my husband than I do. Well, I tell you that Alastair came back to me after six months probation with fifty thousand pounds in his pocket instead of the penal servitude he richly deserved. That man's luck is extraordinary. He always wins. He wins at tennis. He wins at boxing. He won me, the richest heiress in England.

SAGAMORE. But you were a consenting party. If not, why did you put him to the test? Why did you give him the hundred and fifty to try his luck with?

EPIFANIA. Boxing.

SAGAMORE. Boxing?

EPIFANIA. His boxing fascinated me. My father held that women should be able to defend themselves. He made me study Judo.

SAGAMORE. Judo? Do you mean Hebrew?

EPIFANIA. Hebrew! Nonsense! Judo is what ignorant people call jujitsu. I could throw you through that window as easily as you handed me that rotten chair.

SAGAMORE. Oh! Japanese wrestling. Rather a rough sport for a lady, isnt it?

EPIFANIA. How dare you call Judo a sport? It is a religion.

SAGAMORE [*collapsing*] Forgive me. Go on with your story. And please break it to me as gently as you can. I have never had a client like you before.

EPIFANIA. You never will again.

SAGAMORE. I dont doubt it for a moment. Now tell me: where does Alastair come in?

EPIFANIA. I saw him win an amateur heavy weight championship. He has a solar plexus punch that no other boxer can withstand.

SAGAMORE. And you married a man because he had a superlative solar plexus punch!

EPIFANIA. Well, he was handsome. He stripped well, unlike many handsome men. I am not insusceptible to sex appeal, very far from it.

SAGAMORE [*hastily*] Oh quite, quite: you need not go into details.

EPIFANIA. I will if I like. It is your business as a solicitor to know the details. I made a very common mistake. I thought that this irresistible athlete would be an ardent lover. He was nothing of the kind. All his ardor was in his fists. Never shall I forget the day—it was during our honeymoon—when his coldness infuriated me to such a degree that I went for him with my fists. He knocked me out with that abominable punch in the first exchange. Have you ever been knocked out by a punch in the solar plexus?

SAGAMORE. No, thank heaven. I am not a pugilist.

EPIFANIA. It does not put you to sleep like a punch on the jaw. When he saw my face distorted with agony and my body writhing on the floor, he was horrified. He said he did it automatically— that he always countered that way, by instinct. I almost respected him for it.

SAGAMORE. Then why do you want to get rid of him?

EPIFANIA. I want to get rid of myself. I want to punish myself for making a mess of my life and marrying an imbecile. I, Epifania Ognisanti di Parerga, saw myself as the most wonderful woman in England marrying the most wonderful man. And I was only a goose marrying a buck rabbit. What was there for me but death? And now you have put me off it with your fooling; and I dont know what I want. That is a horrible state of mind. I am a woman who must always want something and always get it.

SAGAMORE. An acquisitive woman. Precisely. How splendid! [*The telephone rings. He rises*]. Excuse me. [*He goes to the table and listens*] Yes? . . . [*Hastily*] One moment. Hold the line. [*To Epifania*] Your husband is downstairs, with a woman. They want to see me.

EPIFANIA [*rising*] That woman! Have them up at once.

SAGAMORE. But can I depend on you to control yourself?

EPIFANIA. You can depend on Alastair's fists. I must have a look at Seedystockings. Have them up, I tell you.

SAGAMORE [*into the telephone*] Send Mr Fitzfassenden and the lady up.

EPIFANIA. We shall see now the sort of woman for whom he has deserted ME!

SAGAMORE. I am thrilled. I expect something marvellous.

EPIFANIA. Dont be a fool. Expect something utterly common.

Alastair Fitzfassenden and Patricia Smith come in. He is a splendid athlete, with most of his brains in his muscles. She is a pleasant quiet little woman of the self-supporting type. She makes placidly for the table, leaving Alastair to deal with his wife.

ALASTAIR. Eppy! What are you doing here? [*To Sagamore*] Why didnt you tell me?

EPIFANIA. Introduce the female.

PATRICIA. Patricia Smith is my name, Mrs Fitzfassenden.

EPIFANIA. That is not how you sign your letters, I think.

ALASTAIR. Look here, Eppy. Dont begin making a row—

EPIFANIA. I was not speaking to you. I was speaking to the

woman.

ALASTAIR [*losing his temper*] You have no right to call her a woman.

PATRICIA. Now, now, Ally: you promised me—

EPIFANIA. Promised you! What right had he to promise you? How dare he promise you? How dare you make him promise you?

ALASTAIR. I wont have Polly insulted.

SAGAMORE [*goodhumoredly*] You dont mind, Miss Smith, do you?

PATRICIA [*unconcerned*] Oh, I dont mind. My sister goes on just like that.

EPIFANIA. Your sister! You presume to compare your sister to me!

PATRICIA. Only when she goes off at the deep end. You mustnt mind me: theres nothing like letting yourself go if you are built that way. Introduce me to the gentleman, Ally.

ALASTAIR. Oh, I forgot. Julius Sagamore, my solicitor. An old pal. Miss Smith.

EPIFANIA. Alias Polly Seedystockings.

PATRICIA. Thats only my pet name, Mr Sagamore. Smith is the patronymic, as dear wise old father says.

EPIFANIA. She sets up a wise father! This is the last straw.

SAGAMORE. Do sit down, Miss Smith, wont you? [*He goes to fetch a chair from the wall*].

PATRICIA [*contemplating the wrecked chair*] Hallo! Whats happened to the chair?

EPIFANIA. *I* have happened to the chair. Let it be a warning to you.

Sagamore places the chair for Patricia next the table. Alastair shoves the broken chair back out of the way with his foot; fetches another from the wall; and is about to sit on it next Patricia when Epifania sits on it and motions him to her own chair, so that she is seated between the two, Patricia on her left, Alastair on her right. Sagamore goes back to his official place at the table.

PATRICIA. You see, Mr Sagamore, it's like this. Alastair—

EPIFANIA. You need not explain. I have explained everything

to Mr Sagamore. And you will please have the decency in his presence and in mine to speak of my husband as Mr Fitzfassenden. His Christian name is no business of yours.

ALASTAIR [*angry*] Of course, Eppy, if you wont let anybody speak—

EPIFANIA. I am not preventing you nor anybody from speaking. If you have anything to say for yourself, say it.

PATRICIA. I am sorry. But it's such a long name. In my little circle everyone calls him just Ally.

EPIFANIA [*her teeth on edge*] You hear this, Mr Sagamore! My husband is called "Ally" by these third rate people! What right have they to speak of him at all? Am I to endure this?

PATRICIA [*soothingly*] Yes: we know you have to put up with a lot, deary;—

EPIFANIA [*stamping*] Deary!!!

PATRICIA [*continuing*]—but thats what the world is like.

EPIFANIA. The world is like that to people who are like that. Your world is not my world. Every woman has her own world within her own soul. Listen to me, Mr Sagamore. I married this man. I admitted him to my world, the world which my imagination had peopled with heroes and saints. Never before had a real man been permitted to enter it. I took him to be hero, saint, lover all in one. What he really was you can see for yourself.

ALASTAIR [*jumping up with his fists clenched and his face red*] I am damned if I stand this.

EPIFANIA [*rising and facing him in the pose of a martyr*] Yes: strike me. Shew her your knock-out punch. Let her see how you treat women.

ALASTAIR [*baffled*] Damn! [*He sits down again*].

PATRICIA. Dont get rattled, Ally: you will only put yourself in the wrong before Mr Sagamore. I think youd better go home and leave me to have it out with her.

EPIFANIA. Will you have the goodness not to speak of me as "her"? I am Mrs Fitzfassenden. I am not a pronoun. [*She resumes her seat haughtily*].

PATRICIA. Sorry; but your name is such a tonguetwister. Mr

Sagamore: dont you think Ally had better go? It's not right that we should sit here arguing about him to his face. Besides, he's worn out: he's hardly slept all night.

EPIFANIA. How do you know that, pray?

PATRICIA. Never mind how I know it. I do.

ALASTAIR. It was quite innocent; but where could I go to when you drove me out of the house by your tantrums?

EPIFANIA [*most unexpectedly amused*] You went to her?

ALASTAIR. I went to Miss Smith: she's not a pronoun, you know. I went where I could find peace and kindness, to my good sweet darling Polly. So there!

EPIFANIA. I have no sense of humor; but this strikes me as irresistibly funny. You actually left ME to spend the night in the arms of Miss Seedystockings!

ALASTAIR. No, I tell you. It was quite innocent.

EPIFANIA [*to Patricia*] Was he in your arms or was he not?

PATRICIA. Well, yes, of course he was for a while. But not in the way you mean.

EPIFANIA. Then he is even a more sexless fish than I took him for. But really a man capable of flouncing out of the house when I was on the point of pardoning him and giving him a night of legitimate bliss would be capable of any imbecility.

ALASTAIR. Pardoning me! Pardoning me for what? What had I done when you flew out at me?

EPIFANIA. I did not fly out at you. I have never lost my dignity even under the most insufferable wrongs.

ALASTAIR. You hadnt any wrongs. You drove me out of the house—

EPIFANIA. I did not. I never meant you to go. It was abominably selfish of you. You had your Seedystockings to go to; but I had nobody. Adrian was out of town.

SAGAMORE. Adrian! This is a new complication. Who is Adrian?

PATRICIA. Adrian is Mrs Fitzfassenden's Sunday husband, Mr Sagamore.

EPIFANIA. My what, did you say?

PATRICIA. Your Sunday husband. You understand. What Mr Adrian Blenderbland is to you, as it were. What Ally is to me.

SAGAMORE. I dont quite follow. What is Mr Blenderbland to you, Mrs Fitzfassenden, if I may ask?

EPIFANIA. Well, he is a gentleman with whom I discuss subjects that are beyond my husband's mental grasp, which is extremely limited.

ALASTAIR. A chap that sets up to be an intellectual because his father was a publisher! He makes up to Eppy and pretends to be in love with her because she has a good cook; but I tell her he cares for nothing but his food. He always calls at mealtimes. A bellygod, I call him. And I am expected to put up with him. But if I as much as look at Polly! Oh my!

EPIFANIA. The cases are quite different. Adrian worships the ground I tread on: that is quite true. But if you think that Seedystockings worships the ground you tread on, you flatter yourself grossly. She endures you and pets you because you buy stockings for her, and no doubt anything else she may be short of.

PATRICIA. Well, I never contradict anyone, because it only makes trouble. And I am afraid I do cost him a good deal; for he likes me to have nice things that I cant afford.

ALASTAIR [affectionately] No, Polly: you dont. Youre as good as gold. I'm always pressing things on you that you wont take. Youre a jolly sight more careful of my money than I am myself.

EPIFANIA. How touching! You are the Sunday wife, I suppose.

PATRICIA. No: I should say that you are the Sunday wife, Mrs Fitzfassenden. It's I that have to look after his clothes and make him get his hair cut.

EPIFANIA. Surely the creature is intelligent enough to do at least that much for himself.

PATRICIA. You dont understand men: they get interested in other things and neglect themselves unless they have a woman to look after them. You see, Mr Sagamore, it's like this. There are two sorts of people in the world: the people anyone can live with and the people that no one can live with. The people that no one can live with may be very goodlooking and vital and splendid and temperamental and romantic and all that; and they can make a man or woman happy for half an hour when they are pleased with themselves and disposed to be agreeable; but if you try to live with them they just eat up your whole life running after them or quarrelling or attending to them one way or another: you cant call your soul your own. As Sunday husbands and wives, just to have a good tearing bit of lovemaking with, or a blazing row, or mostly one on top of the other, once a month or so, theyre all right. But as everyday partners theyre just impossible.

EPIFANIA. So I am the Sunday wife. [*To Patricia, scornfully*] And what are you, pray?

PATRICIA. Well, I am the angel in the house, if you follow me.

ALASTAIR [*blubbering*] You are, dear: you are.

EPIFANIA [*to Patricia*] You are his doormat: thats what you are.

PATRICIA. Doormats are very useful things if you want the house kept tidy, dear.

The telephone rings. Sagamore attends to it.

SAGAMORE. Yes? . . . Did you say Blenderbland?

EPIFANIA. Adrian! How did he know I was here?

SAGAMORE. Ask the gentleman to wait. [*He hangs up the receiver*]. Perhaps you can tell me something about him, Mrs Fitzfassenden. Is he the chairman of Blenderbland's Literary Pennyworths?

EPIFANIA. No. That is his father, who created the business. Adrian is on the board; but he has no business ability. He is on fifteen boards of directors on the strength of his father's reputation, and has never, as far as I know, contributed an idea to any of them.

ALASTAIR. Be fair to him, Eppy. No man in London knows how to order a dinner better. Thats what keeps him at the top in the city.

SAGAMORE. Thank you: I think I have his measure sufficiently. Shall I have him up?

EPIFANIA. Certainly. I want to know what he is doing here.

ALASTAIR. I dont mind. You understand, of course, that I am not supposed to know anything of his relations with my wife, whatever they may be.

EPIFANIA. They are perfectly innocent, so far. I am not quite convinced that I love Adrian. He makes himself agreeable: that is all.

SAGAMORE [*into the telephone*] Send Mr Blenderbland up. [*He hangs up the instrument*].

ALASTAIR [*to Patricia*] You will now see the blighter who has cut me out with Eppy.

PATRICIA. I cant imagine any man cutting you out with any woman, dear.

EPIFANIA. Will you be good enough to restrain your endearments when he comes in?

Adrian Blenderbland, an imposing man in the prime of life, bearded in the Victorian literary fashion, rather handsome, and well dressed, comes in. Sagamore rises. Adrian is startled when he sees the company, but recovers his aplomb at once, and advances smiling.

ADRIAN. Hallo! Where have we all come from? Good morning, Mrs Fitzfassenden. How do, Alastair? Mr Sagamore, I presume. I did not know you were engaged.

SAGAMORE. Your arrival is quite opportune, sir. Will you have the goodness to sit down? [*He takes a chair from the wall and places it at the table, on his own right and Patricia's left*].

ADRIAN [*sitting down*] Thank you. I hope I am not interrupting this lady.

PATRICIA. Not at all. Dont mind me.

SAGAMORE [*introducing*] Miss Smith, an intimate friend of Mr Fitzfassenden.

PATRICIA. Pleased to meet you, I'm sure.

Adrian bows to her; then turns to Sagamore.

ADRIAN. The fact is, Mrs Fitzfassenden mentioned your name to me in conversation as her choice of a new solicitor. So I thought I could not place myself in better hands.

SAGAMORE [*bowing*] Thank you, sir. But—excuse me—had you not a solicitor of your own?

ADRIAN. My dear Mr Sagamore: never be content with a single opinion. When I feel ill I always consult at least half a dozen doctors. The variety of their advice and prescriptions convinces me that I had better cure myself. When a legal point arises I consult six solicitors, with much the same—

EPIFANIA. Adrian: I have no sense of humor; and you know how it annoys me when you talk the sort of nonsense that is supposed to be funny. Did you come here to consult Mr Sagamore about me?

ADRIAN. I did. But of course I expected to find him alone.

SAGAMORE. Has the matter on which you wish to consult me any reference to Mr Fitzfassenden's family circle?

ADRIAN. It has.

SAGAMORE. Is it of such a nature that sooner or later it will have to be discussed with all the adult members of that circle?

ADRIAN. Well, yes: I suppose so. But hadnt we better talk it over a little in private first?

EPIFANIA. You shall do nothing of the sort. I will not have my affairs discussed by anybody in public or in private. They concern myself alone.

ADRIAN. May I not discuss my own affairs?

EPIFANIA. Not with my solicitor. I will not have it.

ALASTAIR. Now she is off at the deep end again. We may as well go home.

EPIFANIA [restlessly rising] Oh, the deep end! the deep end! What is life if it is not lived at the deep end? Alastair: you are a tadpole. [She seizes his head and ruffles his hair as she passes him].

ALASTAIR. Dont do that. [He tries to smooth his hair].

EPIFANIA [to Patricia] Smooth it for him, angel in the house.

PATRICIA [moving to Epifania's chair and doing so] You shouldnt make a sight of him like that.

SAGAMORE. Mr Fitzfassenden: why did you marry Mrs Fitzfassenden?

EPIFANIA. Why!!! Does that require any explanation? I have told you why I married him.

ALASTAIR. Well, though you mightnt think it, she can be frightfully fascinating when she really wants to be.

EPIFANIA. Why might he not think it? What do you mean?

ALASTAIR. He knows what I mean.

EPIFANIA. Some silly joke, I suppose.

ADRIAN. Dont be absurd, Fitzfassenden. Your wife is the most adorable woman on earth.

EPIFANIA. Not here, Adrian. If you are going to talk like that, take me away to some place where we can be alone.

ALASTAIR. Do, for heaven's sake, before she drives us all crazy.

SAGAMORE. Steady! steady! I hardly know where I am. You are all consulting me; but none of you has given me any instructions. Had you not better all be divorced?

EPIFANIA. What is the creature to live on? He has nothing: he would have had to become a professional boxer or tennis player if his uncle had not pushed him into an insurance office, where he was perfectly useless.

ALASTAIR. Look here, Eppy: Sagamore doesnt want to hear all this.

EPIFANIA. He does. He shall. Be silent. When Alastair proposed to me—he was too great an idiot to comprehend his own audacity—I kept my promise to my father. I handed him a cheque for a hundred and fifty pounds. "Make that into fifty thousand within six months" I said "and I am yours."

ADRIAN. You never told me this.

EPIFANIA. Why should I? It is a revolting story.

ALASTAIR. What is there revolting about it? Did I make good or did I not? Did I go through hell to get that money and win you or did I not?

ADRIAN [amazed] Do I understand you to say, Alastair, that you made fifty thousand pounds in six months?

ALASTAIR. Why not?

EPIFANIA. You may well look incredulous, Adrian. But he did. Yes: this imbecile made fifty thousand pounds and won Epifania Ognisanti di Parerga for his bride. You will not believe me when I tell you that the possession of all that money, and the consciousness of having made it himself, gave him a sort of greatness. I am impulsive: I kept my word and married him instantly. Then, too late, I found out how he had made it.

ALASTAIR. Well, how did I make it? By my own brains.

EPIFANIA. Brains! By your own folly, your ignorance, your criminal instincts, and the luck that attends the half-witted. You won my hand, for which all Europe was on its knees to me. What you deserved was five years penal servitude.

ALASTAIR. Five years! Fifteen, more likely. That was what I risked for you. And what did I get by it? Life with you was worse than any penal servitude.

EPIFANIA. It would have been heaven to you if Nature had fitted you for such a companionship as mine. But what was it for me? No man had been good enough for me. I was like a princess in a fairy tale offering all men alive my hand and fortune if they could turn my hundred and fifty pound cheque into fifty thousand within six months. Able men, brilliant men, younger sons of the noblest families either refused the test or failed. Why? Because they were too honest or too proud. This thing succeeded; and I found myself tied for life to an insect.

ALASTAIR. You may say what you like; but you were just as much in love with me as I was with you.

EPIFANIA. Well, you were young; you were well shaped; your lawn tennis was outstanding; you were a magnificent boxer; and I was excited by physical contact with you.

SAGAMORE. Is it necessary to be so very explicit, Mrs Fitz-fassenden?

EPIFANIA. Julius Sagamore: you may be made of sawdust; but I am made of flesh and blood. Alastair is physically attractive: that is my sole excuse for having married him. Will you have the face to pretend that he has any mental charm?

ADRIAN. But how did he make the fifty thousand pounds? Was it on the Stock Exchange?

EPIFANIA. Nonsense! the creature does not know the difference between a cumulative preference and a deferred ordinary. He would not know even how to begin.

ADRIAN. But how did he begin? My bank balance at present is somewhere about a hundred and fifty. I should very much like to know how to make it up to fifty thousand. You are so rich,

Epifania, that every decent man who approaches you feels like a needy adventurer. You dont know how a man to whom a hundred pounds is a considerable sum feels in the arms of a woman to whom a million is mere pin money.

EPIFANIA. Nor do you know what it feels like to be in the arms of a man and know that you could buy him up twenty times over and never miss the price.

ADRIAN. If I give you my hundred and fifty pounds, will you invest it for me?

EPIFANIA. It is not worth investing. You cannot make money on the Stock Exchange until your weekly account is at least seventy thousand. Do not meddle with money, Adrian: you do not understand it. I will give you all you need.

ADRIAN. No, thank you: I should lose my self-respect. I prefer the poor man's luxury of paying for your cabs and flowers and theatre tickets and lunches at the Ritz, and lending you all the little sums you have occasion for when we are together.

The rest all stare at this light on Epifania's habits.

EPIFANIA. It is quite true: I never have any pocket money: I must owe you millions in odd five pound notes. I will tell my bankers that you want a thousand on account.

ADRIAN. But I dont. I love lending you fivers. Only, as they run through my comparatively slender resources at an appalling rate, I should honestly like a few lessons from Alastair in the art of turning hundreds into tens of thousands.

EPIFANIA. His example would be useless to you, Adrian, because Alastair is one of Nature's marvels; and there is nothing marvellous about you except your appetite. Listen. On each of his birthdays his aunt had presented him with a gramophone record of the singing of the celebrated tenor Enrico Caruso. Now it so happens that Nature, in one of her most unaccountable caprices, has endowed Alastair with a startlingly loud singing voice of almost supernatural range. He can sing high notes never before attained by mortal man. He found that he could imitate gramophone records with the greatest facility; and he became convinced that he could make a fortune as an operatic tenor. The first use he made of my money was to give fifty pounds to the manager of some trumpery little opera company which was then on its last legs in the suburbs to allow him to appear for one night in one of Caruso's most popular roles. He actually took me to hear his performance.

ALASTAIR. It wasnt my fault. I can sing Caruso's head off. It was a plot. The regular tenor of the company: a swine that could hardly reach B flat without breaking his neck, paid a lot of blackguards to go into the gallery and boo me.

EPIFANIA. My dear Alastair, the simple truth is that Nature, when she endowed you with your amazing voice, unfortunately omitted to provide you with a musical ear. You can bellow loudly enough to drown ten thousand bulls; but you are always at least a quarter tone sharp or flat as the case may be. I laughed until I fell on the floor of my box in screaming hysterics. The audience hooted and booed; but they could not make themselves heard above your roaring. At last the chorus dragged you off the stage; and the regular tenor finished the performance only to find that the manager had absconded with my fifty pounds and left the whole company penniless. The prima donna was deaf in the left ear, into which you had sung with all your force. I had to pay all their salaries and send them home.

ALASTAIR. I tell you it was a plot. Why shouldnt people like my singing? I can sing louder than any tenor on the stage. I can sing higher.

EPIFANIA. Alastair: you cannot resist a plot when the whole world is a party to it.

ADRIAN. Still, this does not explain how Alastair made the fifty thousand pounds.

EPIFANIA. I leave him to tell that disgraceful tale himself. I believe he is proud of it. [*She sits down disdainfully in the vacant chair*].

ALASTAIR. Well, it worked out all right. But it was a near thing, I tell you. What I did was this. I had a hundred pounds left after the opera stunt. I met an American. I told him I was crazy about a woman who wouldnt marry me unless I made fifty thousand in six months, and that I had only a hundred pounds in the world. He jumped up and said "Why, man alive, if you have a hundred you can open a bank account and get a cheque book." I said "What good is a cheque book?" He said "Are we partners, fifty fifty?" So I said yes: what else could I say? That very day we started in. We lodged the money and got a book of a hundred cheques. We took a theatre. We engaged a first rate cast. We got a play. We got a splendid production: the scenery was lovely: the girls were lovely: the principal woman was an angry-eyed creature with a queer foreign voice and a Hollywood accent, just the sort the public loves. We never asked the price of anything: we just went in up to our necks for thousands and thousands.

ADRIAN. But how did you pay for all these things?

ALASTAIR. With our cheques, of course. Didnt I tell you we had a cheque book?

ADRIAN. But when the hundred was gone the cheques must have been dishonored.

ALASTAIR. Not one of them. We kited them all. But it was a heartbreaking job.

ADRIAN. I dont understand. What does kiting mean?

SAGAMORE. It is quite simple. You pay for something with a cheque after the banks have closed for the day: if on Saturday or just before a bank holiday all the better. Say the cheque is for a hundred pounds and you have not a penny at the bank. You must then induce a friend or a hotel manager to cash another cheque for one hundred pounds for you. That provides for the previous cheque; but it obliges you, on pain of eighteen months hard labour, to induce another friend or hotel manager to cash another cheque for you for two hundred pounds. And so you go on spending and kiting from hundreds to thousands and from risks of eighteen months imprisonment to five years, ten years, fourteen years even.

ALASTAIR. If you think that was an easy job, just try it yourself: thats all. I dream of it sometimes: it's my worst nightmare. Why, my partner and I never saw that theatre! never saw that play! until the first night: we were signing cheques and kiting them all the time. Of course it was easier after a while, because as we paid our way all right we found it easier to get credit; and the biggest expenses didnt come until after the play was produced and the money was coming in. I could have done it for half the money; but the American could only keep himself up to the excitement of it by paying twice as much as we needed for everything and shoving shares in it on people for nothing but talk. But it didnt matter when the money began to come in. My! how it did come in! The whole town went mad about the angry-eyed woman. It rained money in bucketsful. It went to my head like drink. It went to the American's head. It went to the head of the American's American friends. They bought all the rights: the film rights, the translation rights, the touring rights, all sorts of rights that I never knew existed, and began selling them to one another until everybody in London and New York and Hollywood had a rake-off on them. Then the American bought all the rights back for five hundred thousand dollars, and sold them to an American syndicate for a million. It took six more Americans to do it; and every one of them had to have a rake-off; but all I wanted was fifty thousand pounds; and I cleared out with that and came swanking back to claim Eppy's hand. She thought I was great. I was great: the money made me great: I tell you I was drunk with it: I was another man. You may believe it or not as you like; but my hats were really too small for me.

EPIFANIA. It is quite true. The creature was not used to money; and it transfigured him. I, poor innocent, had no suspicion that money could work such miracles; for I had possessed millions in my cradle; and it meant no more to me than the air I breathed.

SAGAMORE. But just now, when I suggested a divorce, you asked how he was to live. What has become of the fifty thousand pounds?

EPIFANIA. He lost it all in three weeks. He bought a circus with it. He thought everything he touched would turn into gold. I had to liquidate that circus a month later. He was about to turn the wild beasts loose and run away when I intervened. I was down four hundred and thirty pounds sixteen and sevenpence by the transaction.

ALASTAIR. Was it my fault? The elephant got influenza. The Ministry of Health closed me down and wouldnt let me move on because the animals might carry foot-and-mouth disease.

EPIFANIA. At all events, the net result was that instead of his being fifty thousand pounds to the good I was four hundred and thirty pounds to the bad. Instead of bringing me the revenues of a prince and a hero he cost me the allowance of a worm. And now he has the audacity to ask for a divorce.

ALASTAIR. No I dont. It was Sagamore who suggested that. How can I afford to let you divorce me? As your husband I enjoy a good deal of social consideration; and the tradesmen give me unlimited credit.

EPIFANIA. For stockings, among other things.

PATRICIA. Oh [*she weeps*]! Does she pay for them, Ally?

ALASTAIR. Never mind, dear: I have shewn that I can make money when I am put to it; and I will make it again and buy you all the stockings you need out of my own earnings. [*He rises and goes behind her chair to take her cheeks in his hands*]. There, darling: dont cry.

EPIFANIA. There! They think they are married already!

SAGAMORE. But the matter is not in your hands, Mr Fitzfassenden. Mrs Fitzfassenden can divorce you whether you like it or not. The evidence is that on a recent occasion you left your wife and took refuge in the arms of Miss Smith. The Court will give Mrs Fitzfassenden a decree on that.

PATRICIA [*consoled and plucky*] Well, let it. I can support Alastair until he has time to make another fortune. You all think him a fool; but he's a dear good boy; and it just disgusts me the way you all turn against him, and the way his wife treats him as if he were dirt under her feet. What would she be without her money, I'd like to know?

EPIFANIA. Nobody is anybody without money, Seedystockings. My dear old father taught me that. "Stick to your money" he said "and all the other things shall be added unto you." He said it was in the Bible. I have never verified the quotation; but I have never forgotten it. I have stuck to my money; and I shall continue to stick to it. Rich as I am, I can hardly forgive Alastair for letting me down by four hundred and thirty pounds.

ALASTAIR. Sixteen and sevenpence! Stingy beast. But I will pay it.

PATRICIA. You shall, dear. I will sell out my insurance and give it to you.

EPIFANIA. May I have that in writing, Miss Smith?

ALASTAIR. Oh, you ought to be ashamed of yourself, you greedy pig. It was your own fault. Why did you let the elephant go for thirty pounds? He cost two hundred.

SAGAMORE. Do not let us wander from the point.

EPIFANIA. What is the point, pray?

SAGAMORE. The point is that you can obtain a divorce if you wish.

EPIFANIA. I dont wish. Do you think I am going to be dragged through the divorce court and have my picture in the papers with that thing? To have the story of my infatuation told in headlines in every rag in London! Besides, it is convenient to be married. It is respectable. It keeps other men off. It gives me a freedom that I could not enjoy as a single woman. I have become accustomed to a husband. No: decidedly I will not divorce Alastair—at least until I can find a substitute whom I really want.

PATRICIA. You couldnt divorce him unless he chose to let you. Alastair's too much the gentleman to mention it; but you know very well that your own behavior hasnt been so very nunlike that you dare have it shewn up in court.

EPIFANIA. Alastair was the first man I ever loved; and I hope he will not be the last. But legal difficulties do not exist for people with money. At all events, as Alastair cannot afford to divorce me, and I have no intention of divorcing him, the question does not arise. What o'clock is it?

ALASTAIR. I really think, Eppy, you might buy a wrist watch. I have told you so over and over again.

EPIFANIA. Why should I go to the expense of buying a wrist watch when everyone else has one; and I have nothing to do but ask? I have not carried a watch since I lost the key of my father's old repeater.

PATRICIA. It is ten minutes past twelve.

EPIFANIA. Gracious! I have missed my lesson. How annoying!

ALASTAIR. Your lesson? What are you learning now, may I ask?

EPIFANIA. All-in wrestling. When you next indulge in your favorite sport of wife beating, look out for a surprise. What did I come here for, Mr Sagamore?

SAGAMORE. To give me instructions about your will.

ALASTAIR. She makes a new will every time she loses her temper, Sagamore. Jolly good business for you.

EPIFANIA. Do be quiet, Alastair. You forget the dignity of your position as my husband. Mr Sagamore: I have changed my mind about my will. And I shall overlook your attempt to poison me.

SAGAMORE. Thank you.

EPIFANIA. What do I owe you for this abortive consultation?

SAGAMORE. Thirteen and fourpence, if you please.

EPIFANIA. I do not carry money about with me. Adrian: can you lend me thirteen and fourpence?

ADRIAN [puts his hand in his pocket]——

EPIFANIA. Stop. Mr Sagamore: you had better be my family solicitor and send me your bill at the end of the year.

ALASTAIR. Send a County Court summons with it, Sagamore; or you may go whistle for your money.

EPIFANIA. Do hold your tongue, Alastair. Of course I always wait for a summons. It is a simple precaution against paying bills sent in twice over.

SAGAMORE. Quite, Mrs Fitzfassenden. An excellent rule.

EPIFANIA. You are a man of sense, Mr Sagamore. And now I must have some fresh air: this orgy of domesticity has made the room stuffy. Come along, Adrian: we'll drive out into the country somewhere, and lunch there. I know the quaintest little place up the river. Goodbye, Mr Sagamore. Goodbye, Seedy: take care of Alastair for me. His good looks will give you a pleasing sensation down your spine. [She goes out].

SAGAMORE [as Adrian is following her out] By the way, Mr Blenderbland, what did you come for?

ADRIAN. I totally forget. I dont feel equal to any more this morning. [*He goes out without further salutations*].

SAGAMORE [*to Alastair*] Your wife is a most extraordinary lady.

ALASTAIR [*utters a stifled howl*]!

PATRICIA. He cant find words for her, poor dear.

SAGAMORE. And now, Mr Fitzfassenden, may I ask what you came to consult me about?

ALASTAIR. I dont know. After ten minutes of Eppy I never do know whether I am standing on my head or my heels.

PATRICIA. It was about a separation. Pull yourself together a bit, dear.

ALASTAIR. Separation! You might as well try to separate yourself from a hurricane. [*He becomes sententious*]. Listen to me, Sagamore. I am one of those unfortunate people—you must know a lot of them—I daresay many of them have sat in this chair and talked to you as I am now talking to you—

SAGAMORE [*after waiting in vain for a completion of the sentence*] Yes? You were saying—?

PATRICIA. Dont wander, Ally. Tell Mr Sagamore what sort of people.

ALASTAIR. The people that have bitten off more than they can chew. The ordinary chaps that have married extraordinary women. The commonplace women that have married extraordinary men. They all thought it was a splendid catch for them. Take my advice, Sagamore: marry in your own class. Dont misunderstand me: I dont mean rank or money. What I mean—what I mean—

PATRICIA [*coming to the rescue*] What he means is that people who marry should think about the same things and like the same things. They shouldnt be over oneanother's heads, if you follow me.

SAGAMORE. Perfectly. May I take it that Alastair made that mistake, and that later on (too late, unfortunately) he discovered in you a—shall I say a soul mate?

ALASTAIR. No: that sounds silly. Literary, you know.

PATRICIA. More of a mind mate, I should call it.

SAGAMORE. Precisely. Thank you. A mind mate with whom he could be thoroughly comfortable.

ALASTAIR [*grasping Sagamore's hand fervently*] Thank you, Sagamore: you are a real friend. Youve got it exactly. Think over it for us. Come on, Seedy darling: we mustnt waste a busy man's time.

He goes out, leaving Patricia and Sagamore alone together. She rises and goes to the table.

PATRICIA. Mr Sagamore: youll stand by us, wont you? Youll save Ally from that awful woman. Youll save him for me.

SAGAMORE. I'm afraid I cant control her, Miss Smith. Whats worse, I'm afraid she can control me. It's not only that I cant afford to offend so rich a client. It's that her will paralyzes mine. It's a sort of genius some people have.

PATRICIA. Dont you be afraid of her, Mr Sagamore. She has a genius for making money. It's in her family. Money comes to her. But I have my little bit of genius too; and she cant paralyze me.

SAGAMORE. And what have you a genius for, Miss Smith, if I may ask?

PATRICIA. For making people happy. Unhappy people come to me just as money comes to her.

SAGAMORE [*shaking his head*] I cant think that your will is stronger than hers, Miss Smith.

PATRICIA. It isnt, Mr Sagamore. I have no will at all. But I get what I want, somehow. Youll see.

ALASTAIR [*outside, shouting*] Seedy! Come on!

PATRICIA. Coming, darling. [*To Sagamore*] Goodbye, Mr Sagamore [*they shake hands quickly. She hurries to the door*]. Youll see. [*She goes out*].

SAGAMORE [*to himself*] I think I shall wait and see.

He resumes his morning's work.

ACT II

A dismal old coffee room in an ancient riverside inn. An immense and hideous sideboard of the murkiest mahogany stretches across the end wall. Above it hang, picturewise, two signboards, nearly black with age: one shewing the arms of the lord of the manor, and the other a sow standing upright and playing a flageolet. Underneath the sow is inscribed in tall letters THE PIG & WHISTLE. Between these works of art is a glass case containing an enormous stuffed fish, certainly not less than a century old.

At right angles to the sideboard, and extending nearly the whole length of the room, are two separate long tables, laid for lunch for about a dozen people each. The chairs, too close together, are plain wooden ones, hard and uncomfortable. The cutlery is cheap kitchen ware, with rickety silver cruets and salt cellars to keep up appearances. The table cloths are coarse, and are not fresh from the laundry.

The walls are covered with an ugly Victorian paper which may have begun as a design of dull purple wreaths on a dark yellow background, but is now a flyblown muck of no describable color. On the floor a coarse drugget, very old. The door, which stands wide open and has COFFEE ROOM inscribed on it, is to the right of anyone contemplating the sideboard from the opposite end of the room. Next the door an old fashioned hatstand flattens itself against the wall; and on it hang the hat and light overcoat of Mr Adrian Blenderbland.

He, with Epifania, is seated at the end of the table farthest from the door. They have just finished a meal. The cheese and biscuits are still on the table. She looks interested and happy. He is in the worst of tempers.

EPIFANIA. How jolly!

ADRIAN [*looking round disparagingly*] I must be a very attractive man.

EPIFANIA [*opening her eyes wide*] Indeed! Not that I am denying it; but what has it to do with what I have just said?

159

THE MILLIONAIRESS

ADRIAN. You said "How jolly!" I look round at this rotten old inn trying to pretend that it's a riverside hotel. We have just had a horrible meal of tomato tea called soup, the remains of Sunday's joint, sprouts, potatoes, apple tart and stale American synthetic cheese. If you can suffer this and say "How jolly!" there must be some irresistible attraction present; and I can see nothing that is not utterly repulsive except myself.

EPIFANIA. Dont you like these dear old-world places? I do.

ADRIAN. I dont. They ought all to be rooted up, pulled down, burnt to the ground. Your flat on the Embankment in London cost more to furnish than this place did to build from the cellar to the roof. You can get a decent lunch there, perfectly served, by a word through the telephone. Your luxurious car will whisk you out to one of a dozen first rate hotels in lovely scenery. And yet you choose this filthy old inn and say "How jolly!" What is the use of being a millionairess on such terms?

EPIFANIA. Psha! When I was first let loose on the world with unlimited money, how long do you think it took me to get tired of shopping and sick of the luxuries you think so much of? About a fortnight. My father, when he had a hundred millions, travelled third class and never spent more than ten shillings a day on himself except when he was entertaining people who were useful to him. Why should he? He couldnt eat more than anyone else. He couldnt drink more than anyone else. He couldnt wear more than anyone else. Neither can I.

ADRIAN. Then why do you love money and hate spending it?

EPIFANIA. Because money is power. Money is security. Money is freedom. It's the difference between living on the slope of a volcano and being safe in the garden of the Hesperides. And there is the continual pleasure of making more of it, which is quite easy if you have plenty to start with. I can turn a million into two million much more easily than a poor woman can turn five pounds into ten, even if she could get the five pounds to begin with. It turns itself, in fact.

ADRIAN. To me money is a vulgar bore and a soul destroying worry. I need it, of course; but I dont like it. I never think of it

THE MILLIONAIRESS

when I can possibly help it.

EPIFANIA. If you dont think about money what do you think about? Women?

ADRIAN. Yes, of course; but not exclusively.

EPIFANIA. Food?

ADRIAN. Well, I am not always thinking about my food; but I am rather particular about it. I confess I looked forward to a better lunch than [*indicating the table*] that.

EPIFANIA. Oho! So that is what has put you out of temper, is it?

ADRIAN [*annoyed*] I am not out of temper, I hope. But you promised me a very special treat. You said you had found out the most wonderful place on the river, where we could be ourselves and have a delicious cottage meal in primitive happiness. Where is the charm of this dismal hole? Have you ever eaten a viler lunch? There is not even a private sitting room: anybody can walk in here at any moment. We should have been much more comfortable at Richmond or Maidenhead. And I believe it is raining.

EPIFANIA. Is that my fault?

ADRIAN. It completes your notion of a happy day up the river. Why is it that the people who know how to enjoy themselves never have any money, and the people who have money never know how to enjoy themselves?

EPIFANIA. You are not making yourself agreeable, Adrian.

ADRIAN. You are not entertaining me very munificently, Epifania. For heaven's sake let us get into the car and drive about the country. It is much more luxurious than this hideous coffee room, and more private.

EPIFANIA. I am tired of my car.

ADRIAN. I am not. I wish I could afford one like it.

EPIFANIA. I thought you would enjoy sitting in this crazy out-of-way place talking to me. But I find you are a spoilt old bachelor: you care about nothing but your food and your little comforts. You are worse than Alastair; for he at least could talk about boxing and tennis.

161

M

ADRIAN. And you can talk about nothing but money.

EPIFANIA. And you think money uninteresting! Oh, you should have known my father!

ADRIAN. I am very glad I did not.

EPIFANIA [*suddenly dangerous*] Whats that you say?

ADRIAN. My dear Epifania, if we are to remain friends, I may as well be quite frank with you. Everything you have told me about your father convinces me that though he was no doubt an affectionate parent and amiable enough to explain your rather tiresome father fixation, as Dr Freud would call it, he must have been quite the most appalling bore that ever devastated even a Rotary club.

EPIFANIA [*stunned for a moment by this blasphemy*] My father! You infinite nothingness! My father made a hundred and fifty millions. You never made even half a million.

ADRIAN. My good girl, your father never made anything. I have not the slightest notion of how he contrived to get a legal claim on so much of what other people made; but I do know that he lost four fifths of it by being far enough behind the times to buy up the properties of the Russian nobility in the belief that England would squash the Soviet revolution in three weeks or so. Could anyone have made a stupider mistake? Not I.

EPIFANIA [*springing up*] You rotten thing. [*He rises apprehensively*]. Take that for calling my father a bore. [*She throws him*].

ADRIAN [*picking himself up painfully*] Oh! Restrain yourself. You might have hurt me very seriously.

EPIFANIA. I will hurt you until you wish yourself dead. Scum! Filth! Take that for saying he never made anything. [*She throws him again*].

ADRIAN. Help! help! There is a madwoman here: I shall not be able to hold her single handed. Help! [*He comes behind her and seizes her round the waist*].

EPIFANIA. Vermin! [*She throws him over her shoulder*].

ADRIAN. Police! She is murdering me. She is mad. Help! help! [*He scrambles up and is flying to the door when she overtakes him*].

EPIFANIA. Dirt! Carrion! [*She throws him out head over heels and flings his hat and overcoat after him*].

ADRIAN [*outside, rolling downstairs with appalling bumps*] Oh! Oh! Help! Murder! Police! Oh! [*He faints. Silence*].

EPIFANIA You brute! You have killed me. [*She totters to the nearest chair and sinks into it, scattering the crockery as she clutches the table with her outstretched arms and sprawls on it in convulsions*].

A serious looking middleaged Egyptian gentleman in an old black frock coat and a tarboosh, speaking English too well to be mistaken for a native, hurries in.

THE EGYPTIAN [*peremptorily*] Whats the matter? What is going on here?

EPIFANIA [*raising her head slowly and gazing at him*] Who the devil are you?

THE EGYPTIAN. I am an Egyptian doctor. I hear a great disturbance. I hasten to ascertain the cause. I find you here in convulsions. Can I help?

EPIFANIA. I am dying.

THE DOCTOR. Nonsense! You can swear. The fit has subsided. You can sit up now: you are quite well. Good afternoon.

EPIFANIA. Stop. I am not quite well: I am on the point of death. I need a doctor. I am a rich woman.

THE DOCTOR. In that case you will have no difficulty in finding an English doctor. Is there anyone else who needs my help? I was upstairs. The noise was of somebody falling downstairs. He may have broken some bones. [*He goes out promptly*].

EPIFANIA [*struggling to her feet and calling after him*] Never mind him: if he has broken every bone in his body it is no more than he deserves. Come back instantly. I want you. Come back. Come back.

THE DOCTOR [*returning*] The landlord is taking the gentleman to the Cottage Hospital in your car.

EPIFANIA. In my car! I will not permit it. Let them get an ambulance.

THE DOCTOR. The car has gone. You should be very glad that it is being so useful.

163

EPIFANIA. It is your business to doctor me, not to lecture me.

THE DOCTOR. I am not your doctor: I am not in general practice. I keep a clinic for penniless Mahometan refugees; and I work in the hospital. I cannot attend to you.

EPIFANIA. You can attend to me. You must attend to me. Are you going to leave me here to die?

THE DOCTOR. You are not dying. Not yet, at least. Your own doctor will attend to you.

EPIFANIA. You are my own doctor. I tell you I am a rich woman: doctors' fees are nothing to me: charge me what you please. But you must and shall attend to me. You are abominably rude; but you inspire confidence as a doctor.

THE DOCTOR. If I attended all those in whom I inspire confidence I should be worn out in a week. I have to reserve myself for poor and useful people.

EPIFANIA. Then you are either a fool or a Bolshevik.

THE DOCTOR. I am nothing but a servant of Allah.

EPIFANIA. You are not: you are my doctor: do you hear? I am a sick woman: you cannot abandon me to die in this wretched place.

THE DOCTOR. I see no symptoms of any sickness about you. Are you in pain?

EPIFANIA. Yes. Horrible pain.

THE DOCTOR. Where?

EPIFANIA. Dont cross-examine me as if you didnt believe me. I must have sprained my wrist throwing that beast all over the place.

THE DOCTOR. Which hand?

EPIFANIA [*presenting a hand*] This.

THE DOCTOR [*taking her hand in a businesslike way, and pulling and turning the fingers and wrist*] Nothing whatever the matter.

EPIFANIA. How do you know? It's my hand, not yours.

THE DOCTOR. You would scream the house down if your wrist were sprained. You are shamming. Lying. Why? Is it to make yourself interesting?

EPIFANIA. Make myself interesting! Man: I am interesting.

THE DOCTOR. Not in the least, medically. Are you interesting in any other way?

EPIFANIA. I am the most interesting woman in England. I am Epifania Ognisanti di Parerga.

THE DOCTOR. Never heard of her. Italian aristocrat, I presume.

EPIFANIA. Aristocrat! Do you take me for a fool? My ancestors were moneylenders to all Europe five hundred years ago: we are now bankers to all the world.

THE DOCTOR. Jewess, eh?

EPIFANIA. Christian, to the last drop of my blood. Jews throw half their money away on charities and fancies like Zionism. The stupidest di Parerga can just walk round the cleverest Jew when it comes to moneymaking. We are the only real aristocracy in the world: the aristocracy of money.

THE DOCTOR. The plutocracy, in fact.

EPIFANIA. If you like. I am a plutocrat of the plutocrats.

THE DOCTOR. Well, that is a disease for which I do not prescribe. The only known cure is a revolution; but the mortality rate is high; and sometimes, if it is the wrong sort of revolution, it intensifies the disease. I can do nothing for you. I must go back to my work. Good morning.

EPIFANIA [holding him] But this is your work. What else have you to do?

THE DOCTOR. There is a good deal to be done in the world besides attending rich imaginary invalids.

EPIFANIA. But if you are well paid?

THE DOCTOR. I make the little money I need by work which I venture to think more important.

EPIFANIA [throwing him away and moving about distractedly] You are a pig and a beast and a Bolshevik. It is the most abominable thing of you to leave me here in my distress. My car is gone. I have no money. I never carry money about.

THE DOCTOR. I have none to carry. Your car will return presently. You can borrow money from your chauffeur.

EPIFANIA. You are an unmitigated hippopotamus. You are a Bashibazouk. I might have known it from your ridiculous tarboosh. You should take it off in my presence. [*She snatches it from his head and holds it behind her back*]. At least have the manners to stay with me until my chauffeur comes back.

The motor horn is heard honking.

THE DOCTOR. He has come back.

EPIFANIA. Damn! Cant you wait until he has had his tea and a cigarette?

THE DOCTOR. No. Be good enough to give me back my fez.

EPIFANIA. I wanted to see what you looked like without it. [*She puts it tenderly on his head*]. Listen to me. You are having an adventure. Have you no romance in you? Havnt you even common curiosity? Dont you want to know why I threw that beast downstairs? Dont you want to throw your wretched work to the devil for once and have an afternoon on the river with an interesting and attractive woman?

THE DOCTOR. Women are neither interesting nor attractive to me except when they are ill. I know too much about them, inside and out. You are perfectly well.

EPIFANIA. Liar. Nobody is perfectly well, nor ever has been, nor ever will be. [*She sits down, sulking*].

THE DOCTOR. That is true. You must have brains of a sort. [*He sits down opposite to her*]. I remember when I began as a young surgeon I killed several patients by my operations because I had been taught that I must go on cutting until there was nothing left but perfectly healthy tissue. As there is no such thing as perfectly healthy tissue I should have cut my patients entirely away if the nurse had not stopped me before they died on the table. They died after they left the hospital; but as they were carried away from the table alive I was able to claim a successful operation. Are you married?

EPIFANIA. Yes. But you need not be afraid. My husband is openly unfaithful to me and cannot take you into court if you make love to me. I can divorce him if necessary.

THE DOCTOR. And the man you threw downstairs: who was he? One does not throw one's husband downstairs. Did he make love to you?

EPIFANIA. No. He insulted my father's memory because he was disappointed with his lunch here. When I think of my father all ordinary men seem to me the merest trash. You are not an ordinary man. I should like to see some more of you. Now that you have asked me confidential questions about my family, and I have answered them, you can no longer pretend that you are not my family doctor. So that is settled.

THE DOCTOR. A father fixation, did you say?

EPIFANIA [nods]!

THE DOCTOR. And an excess of money?

EPIFANIA. Only a beggarly thirty millions.

THE DOCTOR. A psychological curiosity. I will consider it.

EPIFANIA. Consider it! You will feel honored, gratified, delighted.

THE DOCTOR. I see. Enormous self-confidence. Reckless audacity. Insane egotism. Apparently sexless.

EPIFANIA. Sexless ! Who told you that I am sexless?

THE DOCTOR. You talk to me as if you were a man. There is no mystery, no separateness, no sacredness about men to you. A man to you is only a male of your species.

EPIFANIA. My species indeed! Men are a different and very inferior species. Five minutes conversation with my husband will convince you that he and I do not belong to the same species. But there are some great men, like my father. And there are some good doctors, like you.

THE DOCTOR. Thank you. What does your regular doctor say about you?

EPIFANIA. I have no regular doctor. If I had I should have an operation a week until there was nothing left of me or of my bank balance. I shall not expect you to maul me about with a stethoscope, if that is what you are afraid of. I have the lungs of a whale and the digestion of an ostrich. I have a clockwork inside. I sleep eight hours like a log. When I want anything I lose my head so completely about it that I always get it.

THE DOCTOR. What things do you want mostly?

EPIFANIA. Everything. Anything. Like a lightning flash. And

THE MILLIONAIRESS

then there is no stopping me.

THE DOCTOR. Everything and anything is nothing.

EPIFANIA. Five minutes ago I wanted you. Now I have got you.

THE DOCTOR. Come! You cannot bluff a doctor. You may want the sun and the moon and the stars; but you cannot get them.

EPIFANIA. That is why I take good care not to want them. I want only what I can get.

THE DOCTOR. Good. A practical intellect. And what do you want at present, for instance?

EPIFANIA. That is the devil of it. There is nothing one can get except more money.

THE DOCTOR. What about more men?

EPIFANIA. More Alastairs! More Blenderblands! Those are not deep wants. At present I want a motor launch.

THE DOCTOR. There is no such thing in this little place.

EPIFANIA. Tell the landlord to stop the first one that comes along and buy it.

THE DOCTOR. Tcha! People will not sell their boats like that.

EPIFANIA. Have you ever tried?

THE DOCTOR. No.

EPIFANIA. I have. When I need a car or a motor boat or a launch or anything like that I buy straight off the road or off the river or out of the harbor. These things cost thousands when they are new; but next day you cannot get fifty pounds for them. Offer £300 for any of them, and the owner dare not refuse: he knows he will never get such an offer again.

THE DOCTOR. Aha! You are a psychologist. This is very interesting.

EPIFANIA. Nonsense! I know how to buy and sell, if that is what you mean.

THE DOCTOR. That is how good psychologists make money.

EPIFANIA. Have you made any?

THE DOCTOR. No. I do not care for money: I care for knowledge.

EPIFANIA. Knowledge is no use without money. Are you

married?

THE DOCTOR. I am married to Science. One wife is enough for me, though by my religion I am allowed four.

EPIFANIA. Four! What do you mean?

THE DOCTOR. I am what you call a Mahometan.

EPIFANIA. Well, you will have to be content with two wives if you marry me.

THE DOCTOR. Oh! Is there any question of that between us?

EPIFANIA. Yes. I want to marry you.

THE DOCTOR. Nothing doing, lady. Science is my bride.

EPIFANIA. You can have Science as well: I shall not be jealous of her. But I made a solemn promise to my father on his deathbed—

THE DOCTOR [*interrupting*] Stop. I had better tell you that I made a solemn promise to my mother on her deathbed.

EPIFANIA. What!!!

THE DOCTOR. My mother was a very wise woman. She made me swear to her that if any woman wanted to marry me, and I felt tempted, I would hand the woman two hundred piastres and tell her that unless she would go out into the world with nothing but that and the clothes she stood in, and earn her living alone and unaided for six months, I would never speak to her again.

EPIFANIA. And if she stood the test?

THE DOCTOR. Then I must marry her even if she were the ugliest devil on earth.

EPIFANIA. And you dare ask me—me, Epifania Ognisanti di Parerga! to submit myself to this test—to any test!

THE DOCTOR. I swore. I have a mother fixation. Allah has willed it so. I cannot help myself.

EPIFANIA. What was your mother?

THE DOCTOR. A washerwoman. A widow. She brought up eleven children. I was the youngest, the Benjamin. The other ten are honest working folk. With their help she made me a man of learning. It was her ambition to have a son who could read and write. She prayed to Allah; and he endowed me with the necessary talent.

EPIFANIA. And you think I will allow myself to be beaten by an old washerwoman?

THE DOCTOR. I am afraid so. You could never pass the test.

EPIFANIA. Indeed! And my father's test for a husband worthy of me?

THE DOCTOR. Oh! The husband is to be tested too! That never occurred to me.

EPIFANIA. Nor to your mother either, it seems. Well, you know better now. I am to give you a hundred and fifty pounds. In six months you are to increase it to fifty thousand. How is that for a test?

THE DOCTOR. Quite conclusive. At the end of the six months I shall not have a penny of it left, praise be to Allah.

EPIFANIA. You confess yourself beaten?

THE DOCTOR. Absolutely. Completely.

EPIFANIA. And you think I am beaten too.

THE DOCTOR. Hopelessly. You do not know what homeless poverty is; and Allah the Compassionate will take care that you never do.

EPIFANIA. How much is two hundred piastres?

THE DOCTOR. At the rate of exchange contemplated by my mother, about thirtyfive shillings.

EPIFANIA. Hand it over.

THE DOCTOR. Unfortunately my mother forgot to provide for this contingency. I have not got thirtyfive shillings. I must borrow them from you.

EPIFANIA. I have not a penny on me. No matter: I will borrow it from the chauffeur. He will lend you a hundred and fifty pounds on my account if you dare ask him. Goodbye for six months. [*She goes out*].

THE DOCTOR. There is no might and no majesty save in Thee, O Allah; but, oh! most Great and Glorious, is this another of Thy terrible jokes?

ACT III

A basement in the Commercial Road. An elderly man, anxious, poor, and ratlike, sits at a table with his wife. He is poring over his accounts. She, on his left, is sewing buttons on a coat, working very fast. There is a pile of coats on the table to her right waiting to have buttons sewn on, and another to her left which she has finished. The table is draped down to the ground with an old cloth. Some daylight comes in down the stone stairs; but does not extend to the side where the couple sit, which is lighted by a small electric bulb on a wire. Between the stairs and the table a dirty old patched curtain hangs in front of an opening into a farther compartment.

A bell tinkles. The woman instantly stops sewing and conceals the piles of coats under the table. Epifania, her dress covered by an old waterproof, and wearing an elaborately damaged hat, comes down the stairs. She looks at the pair; then looks round her; then goes to the curtain and looks through. The old man makes a dash to prevent her, but is too late. He snatches the curtain from her and bars her passage.

THE MAN. What do you want? What are you doing here?

EPIFANIA. I want employment. A woman told me I should find it here. I am destitute.

THE MAN. Thats not the way to get employment: poking your nose into places that dont concern you. Get out. There are no women employed here.

EPIFANIA. You lie. There are six women working in there. Who employs them?

THE MAN. Is that the way to talk to me? You think a lot of yourself, dont you? What do you take me for?

EPIFANIA. A worm.

THE MAN [*making a violent demonstration*]!!

EPIFANIA. Take care. I can use my fists. I can shoot, if necessary.

THE WOMAN [*hurrying to the man and holding him*] Take care, Joe. She's an inspector. Look at her shoes.

EPIFANIA. I am not an inspector. And what is the matter with my shoes, pray?

THE WOMAN [*respectfully*] Well maam, could a woman looking for work at tuppence hapeny an hour afford a west end shoe like that? I assure you we dont employ any women here. We're only caretakers.

EPIFANIA. But I saw six women—

THE MAN [*throwing open the curtain*] Where? Not a soul. Search the whole bloody basement.

THE WOMAN. Hush, hush, Joe: dont speak to the lady like that. You see, maam: theres not a soul.

EPIFANIA. Theres a smell. You have given them a signal to hide. You are breaking the law. Give me some work or I will send a postcard to the Home Office.

THE MAN. Look here, lady. Cant we arrange this? What good will it do you to get me into trouble and shut up my little shop?

EPIFANIA. What good will it do me to say nothing?

THE MAN. Well, what about half a crown a week?

EPIFANIA. I cannot live on half a crown a week.

THE MAN. You can if you look round a bit. There are others, you know.

EPIFANIA. Give me the address of the others. If I am to live by blackmail I must have an extended practice.

THE MAN. Well, if I have to pay I dont see why the others shouldnt too. Will you take half a crown? [*He holds up half a crown*]. Look here! Look at it! Listen to it! [*He rings it on the table*]. It's yours, and another every Wednesday if you keep the inspector off me.

EPIFANIA. It's no use ringing half crowns at me: I am accustomed to them. And I feel convinced that you will pay five shillings if I insist.

THE WOMAN. Oh, maam, have some feeling for us. You dont know the struggle we have to live.

THE MAN [*roughly*] Here: we're not beggars. I'll pay what the business can afford and not a penny more. You seem to know that it can afford five shillings. Well, if you know that, you know that it cant afford any more. Take your five shillings and be damned to you. [*He flings two half crowns on the table*].

THE WOMAN. Oh, Joe, dont be so hasty.

THE MAN. You shut up. You think you can beg a shilling or two off; but you cant. I can size up a tough lot without looking at her shoes. She's got us; and she knows she's got us.

EPIFANIA. I do not like this blackmailing business. Of course if I must I must; but can you not give me some manual work?

THE MAN. You want to get a little deeper into our business, dont you?

EPIFANIA. I am as deep as I can go already. You are employing six women in there. The thing in the corner is a gas engine: that makes you a workshop under the Act. Except that the sanitary arrangements are probably abominable, there is nothing more for me to know. I have you in the hollow of my hand. Give me some work that I can live by or I will have you cleared out like a wasp's nest.

THE MAN. I have a good mind to clear out now and take some place where you wont find me so easy. I am used to changing my address.

EPIFANIA. That is the best card in your hand. You have some business ability. Tell me why you cannot give me work to live by just as you give it, I suppose, to the women I saw in there.

THE MAN. I dont like the people I employ to know too much.

EPIFANIA. I see. They might call in the inspector.

THE MAN. Call in the inspector! What sort of fool are you? They dread the inspector more than I do.

EPIFANIA. Why? Dont they want to be protected?

THE WOMAN. The inspector wouldnt protect them, maam: he'd only shut up the place and take away their job from them. If they thought youd be so cruel as to report them theyd go down on their knees to you to spare them.

THE MAN. You that know such a lot ought to know that a business like this cant afford any luxuries. It's a cheap labor business. As long as I get women to work for their natural wage, I can get along; but no luxuries, mind you. No trade union wages.

173

No sanitary arrangements as you call them. No limewashings every six months. No separate rooms to eat in. No fencing in of dangerous machinery or the like of that: not that I care; for I have nothing but the old gas engine that wouldnt hurt a fly, though it brings me under the blasted Workshop Act as you spotted all right. I have no big machinery; but I have to undersell those that have it. If I put up my prices by a farthing theyd set their machinery going and drop me. You might as well ask me to pay trade union wages as do all that the inspector wants: I should be out of business in a week.

EPIFANIA. And what is a woman's natural wage?

THE MAN. Tuppence hapeny an hour for twelve hours a day.

EPIFANIA. Slavery!

THE WOMAN. Oh no, maam: nobody could call that slavery. A good worker can make from twelve to fifteen shillings a week at it, week in and week out.

THE MAN. Isnt it what the Government paid at the beginning of the war when all the women were called on to do their bit? Do you expect me to pay more than the British Government?

THE WOMAN. I assure you it's the regular and proper wage and always has been, maam.

THE MAN. Like five per cent at the Bank of England it is. This is a respectable business, whatever your inspectors may say.

EPIFANIA. Can a woman live on twelve shillings a week?

THE MAN. Of course she can. Whats to prevent her?

THE WOMAN. Why, maam, when I was a girl in a match factory I had five shillings a week; and it was a godsend to my mother. And a girl who had no family of her own could always find a family to take her in for four and sixpence, and treat her better than if she had been in her father's house.

THE MAN. I can find you a family what'll do it today, in spite of all the damned doles and wages boards that have upset everything and given girls ideas above their station without giving them the means to pamper themselves.

EPIFANIA. Well, I will work even for that, to prove that I can work and support myself. So give me work and have done talking.

THE MAN. Who started talking? You or I?

EPIFANIA. I did. I thank you for the information you have given me: it has been instructive and to the point. Is that a sufficient apology? And now to work, to work. I am in a hurry to get to work.

THE MAN. Well, what work can you do?

THE WOMAN. Can you sew? Can you make buttonholes?

EPIFANIA. Certainly not. I dont call that work.

THE MAN. Well, what sort of work are you looking for?

EPIFANIA. Brain work.

THE MAN. She's dotty!

EPIFANIA. Your work. Managing work. Planning work. Driving work. Let me see what you make here. Tell me how you dispose of it.

THE MAN [to his wife] You had better get on with your work. Let her see it. [To Epifania, whilst the woman pulls out the pile of coats from under the table and sits down resignedly to her sewing] And when youve quite satisfied your curiosity, perhaps youll take that five shillings and go.

EPIFANIA. Why? Dont you find my arrival a pleasant sort of adventure in this den?

THE MAN. I never heard the like of your cheek, not from nobody. [He sits down to his accounts].

EPIFANIA [to the woman, indicating the pile of coats] What do you do with these when they are finished?

THE WOMAN [going on with her work] The man comes with his lorry and takes them away.

EPIFANIA. Does he pay you for them?

THE WOMAN. Oh no. He gives us a receipt for them. Mr Superflew pays us for the receipts at the end of the week.

EPIFANIA. And what does Mr Superflew do with the coats?

THE WOMAN. He takes them to the wholesaler that supplies him with the cloth. The lorry brings us the cloth when it takes away the finished clothes.

EPIFANIA. Why dont you deal directly with the wholesalers?

THE WOMAN. Oh no: that wouldnt be right. We dont know

who they are; and Mr Superflew does. Besides, we couldnt afford a lorry.

EPIFANIA. Does Mr Superflew own the lorry?

THE WOMAN. Oh no: that wouldnt be right. He hires it by the hour from Bolton's.

EPIFANIA. Is the driver always the same man?

THE WOMAN. Yes, of course: always old Tim Goodenough.

EPIFANIA [to the man] Write those names for me: Superflew, Bolton's, Goodenough.

THE MAN. Here! I'm not your clerk, you know.

EPIFANIA. You will be, soon. Do as I tell you.

THE MAN. Well of all the cheek—! [He obeys].

EPIFANIA. When Goodenough comes round next, tell him to tell Bolton's that he has found somebody who will buy the lorry for fourteen pounds. Tell him that if he can induce Bolton's to part from it at that figure you will give him a pound for himself and engage him at half a crown advance on his present wages to drive it just the same old round to the same places. He knows the wholesalers. Mr Superflew is superfluous. We shall collect not only our own stuff but that of all the other sweaters.

THE MAN. Sweaters! Who are you calling sweaters?

EPIFANIA. Man, know thyself. You sweat yourself; you sweat your wife; you sweat those women in there; you live on sweat.

THE MAN. Thats no way to talk about it. It isnt civil. I pay the right wages, same as everybody pays. I give employment that the like of them couldnt make for themselves.

EPIFANIA. You are sensitive about it. I am not. I am going to sweat Mr Superflew out of existence. I am going to sweat Mr Timothy Goodenough instead of allowing Mr Superflew to sweat him.

THE MAN. See here. Does this business belong to me or to you?

EPIFANIA. We shall see. Dare you buy the lorry?

THE MAN. Wheres the money to come from?

EPIFANIA. Where does all money come from? From the bank.

THE MAN. You got to put it there first, havnt you?

EPIFANIA. Not in the least. Other people put it there; and the bank lends it to you if it thinks you know how to extend your business.

THE WOMAN [*terrified*] Oh, Joe, dont trust your money in a bank. No good ever comes out of banks for the likes of us. Dont let her tempt you, Joe.

EPIFANIA. When had you last a holiday?

THE WOMAN. Me! A holiday! We cant afford holidays. I had one on Armistice Day, eighteen years ago.

EPIFANIA. Then it cost a world war and the slaughter of twenty millions of your fellow creatures to give you one holiday in your lifetime. I can do better for you than that.

THE WOMAN. We dont understand that sort of talk here. Weve no time for it. Will you please take our little present and go away?

The bell tinkles.

THE MAN [*rising*] Thats Tim, for the clothes.

EPIFANIA [*masterfully*] Sit down. I will deal with Tim.

She goes out. The man, after a moment of irresolution, sits down helplessly.

THE WOMAN [*crying*] Oh, Joe, dont listen to her: dont let her meddle with us. That woman would spend our little savings in a week, and leave us to slave to the end of our days to make it up again. I cant go on slaving for ever: we're neither of us as young as we were.

THE MAN [*sullen*] What sort of wife are you for a man? You take the pluck out of me every time. Dont I see other men swanking round and throwing money about that they get out of the banks? In and out of banks they are, all day. What do they do but smoke cigars and drink champagne? A five pound note is to them what a penny is to me. Why shouldnt I try their game instead of slaving here for pence and hapence?

THE WOMAN. Cause you dont understand it, Joe. We know our own ways; and though we're poor our ways have never let us down; and they never will if we stick to them. And who would speak to us? who would know us or give us a helping hand in hard times if we began doing things that nobody else does? How would you like to walk down Commercial Road and get nothing but black looks from all your friends and be refused a week's credit in the shops? Joe: Ive gone on in our natural ways all these years without a word of complaint; and I can go on long enough still to make us comfortable when we're too old to see what I'm sewing or you to count the pence. But if youre going to risk everything and put our money in a bank and change our ways I cant go on: I cant go on: itll kill me. Go up and stop her, Joe. Dont let her talk: just put her out. Be a man, darling: dont be afraid of her. Dont break my heart and ruin yourself. Oh, dont sit there dithering: you dont know what she may be doing. Oh! oh! oh! [*She can say no more for sobbing*].

THE MAN [*rising, but not very resolutely*] There! there! Hold your noise: I'm not going to let her interfere with us. I'll put her out all right. [*He goes to the stairs. Epifania comes down*]. Now, missis: lets have an understanding.

EPIFANIA. No understanding is necessary. Tim is sure that Bolton's will take ten pounds for the lorry. Tim is my devoted slave. Make that poor woman stop howling if you can. I am going now. There is not enough work here for me: I can do it all in half a day every week. I shall take a job as scullery maid at a hotel to fill up my time. But first I must go round to the address Tim has given me and arrange that we send them our stuff direct and collect just as Superflew did. When I have arranged everything with them I will come back and arrange everything for you. Meanwhile, carry on as usual. Good morning. [*She goes out*].

THE MAN [*stupefied*] It seems to me like a sort of dream. What could I do?

THE WOMAN [*who has stopped crying on hearing Epifania's allusion to her*] Do what she tells us, Joe. We're like children— [*She begins crying again softly*].

There is nothing more to be said.

ACT IV

The coffee room of The Pig & Whistle, now transmogrified into the lounge of The Cardinal's Hat, a very attractive riverside hotel. The long tables are gone, replaced by several teatables with luxurious chairs round them. The old sideboard, the stuffed fish, the signboards are no more: instead there is an elegant double writing desk for two sitters, divided by stationery cases and electric lamps with dainty shades. Near it is a table with all the illustrated papers and magazines to hand. Farther down the room, towards the side next the door, there is a long well cushioned seat, capable of accommodating three persons. With three chairs at the other side it forms a fireside circle. The old hatstand has gone to its grave with the sideboard. The newly painted walls present an attractive color scheme. The floor is parquetted and liberally supplied with oriental rugs. All the appurtenances of a brand new first class hotel lounge are in evidence.

Alastair, in boating flannels, is sprawling happily on the long seat, reading an illustrated magazine. Patricia, in her gladdest summer rags, is knitting in the middle chair opposite, full of quiet enjoyment.

It is a fine summer afternoon; and the general effect is that of a bank holiday paradise.

ALASTAIR. I say, Seedy, isnt this jolly?

PATRICIA. Yes, darling: it's lovely.

ALASTAIR. Nothing beats a fine week-end on the river. A pull on the water in the morning to give one a good stretch and a good appetite. A good lunch, and then a good laze. What more can any man desire on earth?

PATRICIA. You row so beautifully, Ally. I love to see you sculling. And punting too. You look so well standing up in the punt.

ALASTAIR. It's the quiet of it, the blessed quiet. You are so quiet: I'm never afraid of your kicking up a row about nothing. The river is so smooth. I dont know which is more comforting, you or the river, when I think of myself shooting Niagara three or four times a day at home.

PATRICIA. Dont think of it, darling. It isnt home: this is home.

ALASTAIR. Yes, dear: youre right: this is what home ought to be, though it's only a hotel.

PATRICIA. Well, what more could anyone ask but a nice hotel? All the housekeeping done for us: no trouble with the servants: no rates nor taxes. I have never had any peace except in a hotel. But perhaps a man doesnt feel that way.

The manager of the hotel, a young man, smartly dressed, enters. He carries the hotel register, which he opens and places on the newspaper table. He then comes obsequiously to his two guests.

MANAGER [*between them*] Good afternoon, sir. I hope you find everything here to your liking.

ALASTAIR. Yes, thanks. But what have you done to the old place? When I was here last, a year ago, it was a common pub called The Pig and Whistle.

THE MANAGER. It was so until quite lately, sir. My father kept The Pig and Whistle. So did his forefathers right back to the reign of William the Conqueror. Cardinal Wolsey stopped once for an hour at The Pig and Whistle when his mule cast a shoe and had to go to the blacksmith's. I assure you my forefathers thought a lot of themselves. But they were uneducated men, and ruined the old place by trying to improve it by getting rid of the old things in it. It was on its last legs when you saw it, sir. I was ashamed of it.

ALASTAIR. Well, you have made a first rate job of it now.

THE MANAGER. Oh, it was not my doing, sir: I am only the manager. You would hardly believe it if I were to tell you the story of it. Much more romantic, to my mind, than the old tale about Wolsey. But I mustnt disturb you talking. You will let me know if theres anything I can do to make you quite comfortable.

PATRICIA. I should like to know about the old Pig if it's romantic. If you can spare the time, of course.

THE MANAGER. I am at your service, madam, always.

ALASTAIR. Fire ahead, old man.

THE MANAGER. Well, madam, one day a woman came here and asked for a job as a scullery maid. My poor old father hadnt the nerve to turn her out: he said she might just try for a day or two. So she started in. She washed two dishes and broke six. My poor old mother was furious: she thought the world of her dishes. She had no suspicion, poor soul, that they were ugly and common and old and cheap and altogether out of date. She said that as the girl had broken them she should pay for them if she had to stay for a month and have the price stopped out of her wages. Off went the girl to Reading and came back with a load of crockery that made my mother cry: she said we should be disgraced for ever if we served a meal on such old fashioned things. But the very next day an American lady with a boating party bought them right off the table for three times what they cost; and my poor mother never dared say another word. The scullery maid took things into her own hands in a way we could never have done. It was cruel for us; but we couldnt deny that she was always right.

PATRICIA. Cruel! What was there cruel in getting nice crockery for you?

THE MANAGER. Oh, it wasnt only that, madam: that part of it was easy and pleasant enough. You see all she had to do with the old crockery was to break it and throw the bits into the dustbin. But what was the matter with the old Pig and Whistle was not the old thick plates that took away your appetite. It was the old people it had gathered about itself that were past their work and had never been up to much according to modern ideas. They had to be thrown into the street to wander about for a few days and then go into the workhouse. There was the bar that was served by father and mother: she dressed up to the nines, as she thought, poor old dear, never dreaming that the world was a day older than when she was married. The scullery maid told them the truth about themselves; and it just cut them to pieces; for it was the truth; and I couldnt deny it. The old man had to give in, because he had raised money on his freehold and was at his wits' end to pay the mortgage interest. The next thing we knew, the girl had paid off the mortgage and got the whip hand of us completely. "It's time for you two to sell your freehold and retire:

you are doing no good here" she said.

PATRICIA. But that was dreadful, to root them up like that.

THE MANAGER. It was hard; but it was the truth. We should have had the brokers in sooner or later if we had gone on. Business is business; and theres no room for sentiment in it. And then, think of the good she did. My parents would never have got the price for the freehold that she gave them. Here was I, ashamed of the place, tied to the old Pig and Whistle by my feeling for my parents, with no prospects. Now the house is a credit to the neighborhood and gives more employment than the poor old Pig did in its best days; and I am the manager of it with a salary and a percentage beyond anything I could have dreamt of.

ALASTAIR. Then she didnt chuck you, old man.

THE MANAGER. No, sir. You see, though I could never have made the change myself, I was intelligent enough to see that she was right. I backed her up all through. I have such faith in that woman, sir, that if she told me to burn down the hotel tonight I'd do it without a moment's hesitation. When she puts her finger on a thing it turns into gold every time. The bank would remind my father if he overdrew by five pounds; but the manager keeps pressing overdrafts on her: it makes him miserable when she has a penny to her credit. A wonderful woman, sir: one day a scullery maid, and the next the proprietress of a first class hotel.

PATRICIA. And are the old people satisfied and happy?

THE MANAGER. Well, no: the change was too much for them at their age. My father had a stroke and wont last long, I'm afraid. And my mother has gone a bit silly. Still, it was best for them; and they have all the comforts they care for.

ALASTAIR. Well, thats a very moving tale: more so than you think, old boy, because I happen to know a woman of that stamp. By the way, I telegraphed for a friend of mine to come and spend the week-end with us here: a Mr Sagamore. I suppose you can find a room for him.

THE MANAGER. That will be quite all right, sir, thank you.

PATRICIA. Have you many people in the house this week-end?

THE MANAGER. Less than usual, madam. We have an Egyptian

doctor who takes his meals here: a very learned man I should think: very quiet: not a word to anybody. Then there is another gentleman, an invalid, only just discharged from the Cottage Hospital. The Egyptian doctor recommended our chef to him; and he takes his meals here too. And that is all, madam, unless some fresh visitors arrive.

ALASTAIR. Well, we must put up with them.

THE MANAGER. By the way, sir, I am sorry to trouble you; but you came up this morning without signing the register. I have brought it up. Would you be so good? [*He fetches the register from the table and presents it to Alastair with his fountain pen*].

ALASTAIR [*sitting up and taking it on his knees*] Oh, I am sorry: I forgot. [*He signs*]. There you are. [*He puts up his legs again*].

THE MANAGER. Thanks very much, sir. [*He glances at the register before shutting it. The signature surprises him*]. Oh, indeed, sir! We are honored.

ALASTAIR. Anything wrong?

THE MANAGER. Oh no, sir, nothing wrong: quite the contrary. Mr and Mrs Fitzfassenden. The name is so unusual. Have I the honor of entertaining the celebrated——

ALASTAIR [*interrupting*] Yes: it's all right: I am the tennis champion and the boxing champion and all the rest of it; but I am here for a holiday and I dont want to hear anything more about it.

THE MANAGER [*shutting the book*] I quite understand, sir. I should not have said anything if it were not that the proprietress of this hotel, the lady I told you of, is a Mrs Fitzfassenden.

ALASTAIR [*rising with a yell*] What! Let me out of this. Pack up, Seedy. My bill, please, instantly.

THE MANAGER. Certainly, sir. But may I say that she is not on the premises at present and that I do not expect her this week-end.

PATRICIA. Dont fuss, darling. Weve a perfect right to be in her hotel if we pay our way just like anybody else.

ALASTAIR. Very well: have it your own way. But my week-end is spoilt.

THE MANAGER. Depend on it, she wont come, sir. She is getting tired of paying us unexpected visits now that she knows she can depend on me. [*He goes out, but immediately looks in again to say*] Your friend Mr Sagamore, sir, coming up with the invalid gentleman. [*He holds the door open for Sagamore and Adrian, who come in. Then he goes out, taking the register with him*].

Adrian, who comes first, limps badly on two walking sticks; and his head is bandaged. He is disagreeably surprised at seeing Fitzfassenden and Patricia.

ADRIAN. Alastair! Miss Smith! What does this mean, Sagamore? You never told me who you were bringing me to see: you said two friends. Alastair: I assure you I did not know you were here. Sagamore said some friends who would be glad to see me.

PATRICIA. Well, we are glad to see you, Mr Blenderbland. Wont you sit down?

ALASTAIR. But whats happened to you, old chap? What on earth have you done to yourself?

ADRIAN [*exasperated*] Everyone asks me what I have done to myself. I havnt done anything to myself. I suppose you mean this and this [*he indicated his injuries*]. Well, they are what your wife has done to me. That is why Sagamore should not have brought me here.

ALASTAIR. I say: I am frightfully sorry, old chap.

PATRICIA [*rising solicitously*] Do sit down, Mr Blenderbland. Rest yourself on that couch. [*Arranging cushions*] Dear! dear!

ALASTAIR. Eppy is like that, you know.

ADRIAN. Yes: I know now. But I ought not to be here: Sagamore should not have brought me here.

PATRICIA. But why not? I assure you we're delighted to see you. We dont mind what Mrs Fitzfassenden does.

ADRIAN. But I do. You are most kind; but I cannot claim the privilege of a friend and at the same time be the plaintiff in an action for assault and battery.

ALASTAIR. Yes you can, old chap. The situation is not new. The victims always come to us for sympathy. Make yourself comfortable.

ADRIAN [*reluctantly sitting down and disposing his damaged*

184

limbs along the couch] Well, it's most kind of you; and I really cant stand any longer. But I dont understand why Sagamore should have played such a trick on me. And, of course, on you too.

Patricia returns to her chair, and resumes her knitting.

SAGAMORE [*taking a chair next Patricia on her left*] Well, the truth of the matter is that Blenderbland wont be reasonable; and I thought you two might help me to bring him to his senses.

ADRIAN [*obstinately*] It's no use, Sagamore. Two thousand five hundred. And costs. Not a penny less.

SAGAMORE. Too much. Ridiculous. A jury might give five hundred if there was a clear disablement from earning, or if the defendant had done something really womanly, like throwing vitriol. But you are only a sleeping partner in the firm your father founded: you dont really earn your income. Besides, hang it all! a man accusing a woman of assault!

ALASTAIR. Why didnt you give her a punch in the solar plexus?

ADRIAN. Strike a woman! Impossible.

ALASTAIR. Rot! If a woman starts fighting she must take what she gets and deserves.

PATRICIA. Look at the marks she's left on you, Mr Blenderbland! You shouldnt have put up with it: it only encourages her.

ALASTAIR. Search me for marks: you wont find any. Youd have found a big mark on her the first time she tried it on me. There was no second time.

ADRIAN. Unfortunately I have neither your muscle nor your knowledge of how to punch. But I will take lessons when I get well. And she shall pay for them. Two thousand five hundred. And medical expenses. And costs.

SAGAMORE. And cab fare to the Cottage Hospital, I suppose.

ADRIAN. No: I went in her own car. But now you remind me, I tipped the chauffeur. Now dont misunderstand me. It is not the money. But I wont be beaten by a woman. It's a point of honor: of self-respect.

SAGAMORE. Yes; but how do you arrive at the figure? Why is your honor and self-respect worth two thousand five hundred pounds and not two thousand five hundred millions?

ADRIAN. My brother got two thousand five hundred from the railway company when an electric truck butted into him on the platform at Paddington. I will not let Epifania off with less. It was an unprovoked, brutal, cowardly assault.

SAGAMORE. Was it quite unprovoked? You will not get a jury to swallow that without a peck of salt?

ADRIAN. I have told you over and over again that it was absolutely unprovoked. But the concussion from which I suffered obliterated all consciousness of what happened immediately before the assault: the last thing I can recollect was a quite ordinary conversation about her father's money.

SAGAMORE. So much the worse for you. She can accuse you of anything she likes. And remember: no man can get damages out of a British jury unless he goes into court as a moral man.

ADRIAN. Do you suggest that I am not a moral man?

SAGAMORE. No; but Mrs Fitzfassenden's counsel will if you take her into court.

ADRIAN. Stuff! Would any jury believe that she and I were lovers on the strength of a sprained ankle, a dislocated knee, and a lump on my head the size of an ostrich's egg?

SAGAMORE. The best of evidence against you. It's only lovers that have lovers' quarrels. And suppose she pleads self-defence against a criminal assault!

ADRIAN. She dare not swear to such a lie.

SAGAMORE. How do you know it's a lie? You dont know what happened at the end. You had concussion of the brain.

ADRIAN. Yes: after the assault.

SAGAMORE. But it obliterated your consciousness of what happened before the assault. How do you know what you did in those moments?

ADRIAN. Look here. Are you my solicitor or hers?

SAGAMORE. Fate seems to have made me the solicitor of everybody in this case. If I am forced to throw up either her case or yours, I must throw up yours. How can I afford to lose a client with such an income and such a temper? Her tantrums are worth two or three thousand a year to any solicitor.

ADRIAN. Very well, Sagamore. You see my condition: you know that right and justice are on my side. I shall not forget this.

The manager enters, looking very serious.

THE MANAGER [*to Alastair*] I am extremely sorry, sir. Mrs Fitzfassenden is downstairs with the Egyptian doctor. I really did not expect her.

EPIFANIA [*dashing into the room and addressing herself fiercely to the manager*] You have allowed my husband to bring a woman to my hotel and register her in my name. You are fired. [*She is behind the couch and does not see Adrian. Sagamore rises*].

THE MANAGER. I am sorry, madam: I did not know that the gentleman was your husband. However, you are always right. Do you wish me to go at once or to carry on until you have replaced me?

EPIFANIA. I do not wish you to go at all: you are re-engaged. Throw them both out, instantly.

ALASTAIR. Ha ha ha!

SAGAMORE. Your manager cannot throw Alastair out: Alastair can throw all of us out, if it comes to that. As to Miss Smith, this is a licensed house; and she has as much right to be here as you or I.

EPIFANIA. I will set fire to the hotel if necessary. [*She sees Adrian*]. Hallo! What is this? Adrian here too! What has happened to your head? What are those sticks for? [*To the manager*] Send the doctor here at once. [*To Adrian*] Have you hurt yourself?

The manager hurries out, glad to escape from the mêlée.

ADRIAN. Hurt myself! Hurt myself!!

EPIFANIA. Has he been run over?

ADRIAN. This woman has half killed me; and she asks have I hurt myself! I fell down the whole flight of stairs. My ankle was sprained. My knee was twisted. The small bone of my leg was broken. I ricked my spine. I had to give them a subscription at the Cottage Hospital, where your man took me. I had to go from there to a nursing home: twelve guineas a week. I had to call in three Harley Street surgeons; and none of them knew anything about dislocated knees: they wanted to cut my knee open to see what was the matter with it. I had to take it to a bonesetter; and he charged me fifty guineas.

EPIFANIA. Well, why did you not walk downstairs properly? Were you drunk?

ADRIAN [*suffocating*] I—

SAGAMORE [*cutting in quickly*] He declares that his injuries were inflicted by you when you last met, Mrs Fitzfassenden.

EPIFANIA. By me! Am I a prizefighter? Am I a coalheaver?

ADRIAN. Both.

SAGAMORE. Do you deny that you assaulted him?

EPIFANIA. Of course I deny it. Anything more monstrous I never heard. What happened was that he insulted my father grossly, without the slightest provocation, at a moment when I had every reason to expect the utmost tenderness from him. The blood rushed to my head: the next thing I remember is that I was lying across the table, trembling, dying. The doctor who found me can tell you what my condition was.

ADRIAN. I dont care what your condition was. What condition did your chauffeur find me in?

SAGAMORE. Then neither of you has the least notion of how this affair ended.

ADRIAN. I have medical evidence.

EPIFANIA. So have I.

ADRIAN. Well, we shall see. I am not going to be talked out of my case.

EPIFANIA. What do you mean by your case?

SAGAMORE. He is taking an action against you.

EPIFANIA. An action! Very well: you know my invariable rule. Fight him to the last ditch, no matter what it costs. Take him to the House of Lords if necessary. We shall see whose purse will hold out longest. I will not be blackmailed.

ADRIAN. You think your father's money places you above the law?

EPIFANIA [*flushing*] Again!

She makes for him. Alastair seizes her from behind and whirls her away towards Sagamore; then places himself on guard between her and the couch, balancing his fist warningly.

ALASTAIR. Now! now! now! None of that. Toko, my girl, toko.

SAGAMORE. Toko! What is toko?

ALASTAIR. She knows. Toko is an infallible medicine for calming the nerves. A punch in the solar plexus and a day in bed: thats toko.

EPIFANIA. You are my witness, Mr Sagamore, how I go in fear of my husband's brutal violence. He is stronger than I am: he can batter me, torture me, kill me. It is the last argument of the lower nature against the higher. My innocence is helpless. Do your worst. [*She sits down in Sagamore's chair with great dignity*].

ALASTAIR. Quite safe now, ladies and gentlemen. [*He picks up his illustrated paper, and retires with it to one of the remoter tea-tables, where he sits down to read as quietly as may be*].

ADRIAN [*to Epifania*] Now you know what I felt. It serves you right.

EPIFANIA. Yes: go on. Insult me. Threaten me. Blackmail me. You can all do it with impunity now.

SAGAMORE [*behind her chair*] Dont take it that way, Mrs Fitzfassenden. There is no question of blackmailing or insulting you. I only want to settle this business of Mr Blenderbland's injuries before we go into the matrimonial question.

EPIFANIA. I want to hear no more of Mr Blenderbland and his ridiculous injuries.

SAGAMORE. Do be a little reasonable, Mrs Fitzfassenden. How are we to discuss the compensation due to Mr Blenderbland without mentioning his injuries?

EPIFANIA. There is no compensation due to Mr Blenderbland. He deserved what he got, whatever that was.

SAGAMORE. But he will take an action against you.

EPIFANIA. Take one against him first.

SAGAMORE. What for?

EPIFANIA. For anything; only dont bother me about it. Claim twenty thousand pounds damages. I tell you I will not be black-mailed.

ADRIAN. Neither will I. I am entitled to compensation and I mean to have it.

SAGAMORE [*coming between them*] Steady! steady! please. I cannot advise either of you to go to law; but quite seriously, Mrs Fitzfassenden, Mr Blenderbland is entitled to some compensation. You can afford it.

EPIFANIA. Mr Sagamore: a woman as rich as I am cannot afford anything. I have to fight to keep every penny I possess. Every beggar, every blackmailer, every swindler, every charity, every testimonial, every political cause, every league and brotherhood and sisterhood, every church and chapel, every institution of every kind on earth is busy from morning to night trying to bleed me to death. If I weaken for a moment, if I let a farthing go, I shall be destitute by the end of the month. I subscribe a guinea a year to the Income Tax Payers' Defence League; but that is all: absolutely all. My standing instructions to you are to defend every action and to forestall every claim for damages by a counter-claim for ten times the amount. That is the only way in which I can write across the sky "Hands off My Money."

SAGAMORE. You see, Mr Blenderbland, it's no use. You must withdraw your threat of an action.

ADRIAN. I wont.

SAGAMORE. You will. You must. Mrs Fitzfassenden: he can do nothing against you. Let me make an appeal on his behalf ad misericordiam.

EPIFANIA [*impatiently*] Oh, we are wasting time; and I have more important business to settle. Give him a ten pound note and have done with it.

ADRIAN. A ten pound note!!!

SAGAMORE [*remonstrant*] Oh, Mrs Fitzfassenden!

EPIFANIA. Yes: a ten pound note. No man can refuse a ten pound note if you crackle it under his nose.

SAGAMORE. But he wants two thousand five hundred.

EPIFANIA [*rising stupefied*] Two thou— [*She gasps*].

ADRIAN. Not a penny less.

EPIFANIA [*going past Sagamore to the couch*] Adrian, my child,

I have underrated you. Your cheek, your gluttony, your obstinacy impose respect on me. I threw a half baked gentleman downstairs; and my chauffeur picked him up on the mat a magnificently complete Skunk.

ADRIAN [*furious*] Five thousand for that, Sagamore: do you hear?

SAGAMORE. Please! please! Do keep your temper.

ADRIAN. Keep your own temper. Has she lamed you for life? Has she raised a bump on your head? Has she called you a skunk?

SAGAMORE. No; but she may at any moment.

EPIFANIA [*flinging her arms round him with a whoop of delight*] Ha ha! Ha ha! My Sagamore! My treasure! Shall I give him five thousand on condition that he turns it into a million in six months?

ADRIAN. I will do what I like with it. I will have it unconditionally.

SAGAMORE [*extricating himself gently from Epifania's hug*] Mr Blenderbland: it is a mistake to go into court in the character of a man who has been called a skunk. It makes the jury see you in that light from the start. It is also very difficult for a plaintiff to get sympathy in the character of a man who has been thrashed by a woman. If Mrs Fitzfassenden had stabbed you, or shot you, or poisoned you, that would have been quite in order: your dignity would not have been compromised. But Mrs Fitzfassenden knows better. She knows the privileges of her sex to a hair's breadth and never oversteps them. She would come into court beautifully dressed and looking her best. No woman can be more ladylike—more feminine—when it is her cue to play the perfect lady. Long before we can get the case into the lists the bump on your head will have subsided; your broken bone will have set; and the color will have come back to your cheeks. Unless you can provoke Mrs Fitzfassenden to assault you again the day before the trial—and she is far too clever for that—the chances are a million to one against you.

ALASTAIR [*rising and coming from the other end of the room*] That is so, Blenderbland. You havnt a dog's chance. Next time you see her fist coming in your direction, duck and counter. If

THE MILLIONAIRESS

you dont get that satisfaction you wont get any. [*He sits down next Patricia, on her right*].

PATRICIA. Yes, Mr Blenderbland: Alastair's right. Ask her nicely, and perhaps she'll pay your expenses.

ADRIAN [*sitting up and taking his head in his hands, shaken, almost lachrymose*] Is there any justice for a man against a woman?

SAGAMORE [*sitting beside him to console him*] Believe me: no. Not against a millionairess.

EPIFANIA. And what justice is there for a millionairess, I should like to know?

SAGAMORE. In the courts—

EPIFANIA. I am not thinking of the courts: there is little justice there for anybody. My millions are in themselves an injustice. I speak of the justice of heaven.

ALASTAIR. Oh Lord! Now we're for it. [*He deliberately puts his arm round Patricia's waist*].

EPIFANIA. Alastair: how can you jeer at me? Is it just that I, because I am a millionairess, cannot keep my husband, cannot keep even a lover, cannot keep anything but my money? There you sit before my very eyes, snuggling up to that insignificant little nothingness who cannot afford to pay for her own stockings; and you are happy and she is happy. [*She turns to Adrian*] Here is this suit of clothes on two sticks. What does it contain?

ADRIAN [*broken*] Let me alone, will you?

EPIFANIA. Something that once resembled a man, something that liked lending me five pound notes and never asked me to repay them. Why? Kindness to me? Love of me? No: the swank of a poor man lending to a millionairess. In my divine wrath I smashed him as a child smashes a disappointing toy; and when he was beaten down to his real self I found I was not a woman to him but a bank account with a good cook.

PATRICIA. Thats all very fine, deary; but the truth is that no one can live with you.

EPIFANIA. And anyone can live with you. And apparently you can live with anybody.

ALASTAIR. What Seedy says is God's truth. Nobody could live

192

with you.

EPIFANIA. But why? Why? Why?

SAGAMORE. Do be reasonable, Mrs Fitzfassenden. Can one live with a tornado? with an earthquake? with an avalanche?

EPIFANIA. Yes. Thousands of people live on the slopes of volcanoes, in the track of avalanches, on land thrown up only yesterday by earthquakes. But with a millionairess who can rise to her destiny and wield the power her money gives her, no. Well, be it so. I shall sit in my lonely house, and be myself, and pile up millions until I find a man good enough to be to me what Alastair is to Seedystockings.

PATRICIA. Well, I hope you wont have to wait too long.

EPIFANIA. I never wait. I march on; and when I come upon the things I need I grab them. I grabbed your Alastair. I find that he does not suit me: he beats me—

ALASTAIR. In self-defence. I never raised a hand to you except in self-defence.

EPIFANIA. Yes: you are like the great European Powers: you never fight except in self-defence. But you are two stone heavier than I; and I cannot keep my head at infighting as you can. You do not suit. I throw you to Greedy-Seedy-Stockings: you can punch her to your heart's content. Mr Sagamore: arrange the divorce. Cruelty and adultery.

PATRICIA. But I dont like this: it's not fair to Alastair. Why is he to be divorced instead of you?

EPIFANIA. Mr Sagamore: take an action against Patricia Smith for alienating my husband's affections. Damages twenty thousand pounds.

PATRICIA. Oh! Is such a thing possible, Mr Sagamore?

SAGAMORE. I am afraid it is, Miss Smith. Quite possible.

PATRICIA. Well, my dear old father used to say that in the law courts there is only one way to beat the people who have un-limited money; and that is to have no money at all. You cant get twenty thousand out of me. And call it vanity if you will; but I should rather like the world to know that in my little way I was able to take the best and dearest man in England from the richest woman.

EPIFANIA. Damn your dear old father!

ALASTAIR [*laughing boisterously*] Ha ha! One for you, Eppy. [*He kisses Patricia*].

SAGAMORE [*smiling*] I am afraid the laugh is with old Mr Smith, Mrs Fitzfassenden. Where there is nothing, the king loses his rights.

EPIFANIA. Oh, I can bear no more of this. I will not have my life dragged down to planes of vulgarity on which I cannot breathe. I will live in utter loneliness and keep myself sacred until I find the right man—the man who can stand with me on the utmost heights and not lose his head—the mate created for me in heaven. He must be somewhere.

THE DOCTOR [*appearing at the door*] The manager says I am wanted here. Who wants me?

EPIFANIA. *I* want you. Come here [*she stretches out her hand to him imperiously*].

THE DOCTOR [*coming to her and feeling her pulse*] Something wrong with your blood pressure, eh? [*Amazed*] Ooooh!! I have never felt such a pulse. It is like a slow sledge hammer.

EPIFANIA. Well, is my pulse my fault?

THE DOCTOR. No. It is the will of Allah. All our pulses are part of the will of Allah.

ALASTAIR. Look here, you know, Doc: that wont go down in this country. We dont believe in Allah.

THE DOCTOR. That does not disconcert Allah in the least, my friend. The pulse beats still, slow, strong. [*To Epifania*] You are a terrible woman; but I love your pulse. I have never felt anything like it before.

PATRICIA. Well, just fancy that! He loves her pulse.

THE DOCTOR. I am a doctor. Women as you fancy them are nothing to me but bundles of ailments. But the life! the pulse! is the heartbeat of Allah, save in Whom there is no majesty and no might. [*He drops her hand*].

EPIFANIA. My pulse will never change: this is the love I crave for. I will marry you. Mr Sagamore: see about a special licence the moment you have got rid of Alastair.

THE DOCTOR. It is not possible. We are bound by our vows.

EPIFANIA. Well, have I not passed your mother's test? You shall have an accountant's certificate. I learned in the first half hour of my search for employment that the living wage for a single woman is five shillings a week. Before the end of the week I had made enough to support me for a hundred years. I did it honestly and legitimately. I explained the way in which it was done.

THE DOCTOR. It was not the way of Allah, the Merciful, the Compassionate. Had you added a farthing an hour to the wages of those sweated women, that wicked business would have crashed on your head. You sold it to the man Superflew for the last penny of his savings; and the women still slave for him at one piastre an hour.

EPIFANIA. You cannot change the market price of labor: not Allah himself can do that. But I came to this hotel as a scullery maid: the most incompetent scullery maid that ever broke a dinner service. I am now its owner; and there is no tuppence-hapeny an hour here.

THE DOCTOR. The hotel looks well in photographs; and the wages you pay would be a fortune to a laborer on the Nile. But what of the old people whose natural home this place had become? the old man with his paralytic stroke? the old woman gone mad? the cast out creatures in the workhouse? Was not this preying on the poverty of the poor? Shall I, the servant of Allah, live on such gains? Shall I, the healer, the helper, the guardian of life and the counsellor of health, unite with the exploiter of misery?

EPIFANIA. I have to take the world as I find it.

THE DOCTOR. The wrath of Allah shall overtake those who leave the world no better than they found it.

EPIFANIA. I think Allah loves those who make money.

SAGAMORE. All the evidence is that way, certainly.

THE DOCTOR. I do not see it so. I see that riches are a curse; poverty is a curse; only in the service of Allah is there justice, righteousness, and happiness. But all this talk is idle. This lady has easily fulfilled the condition imposed by my mother. But I have not fulfilled the condition imposed by the lady's father.

EPIFANIA. You need not trouble about that. The six months have not expired. I will shew you how to turn your hundred and fifty pounds into fifty thousand.

THE DOCTOR. You cannot. It is gone.

EPIFANIA. Oh, you cannot have spent it all: you who live like a mouse. There must be some of it left.

THE DOCTOR. Not a penny. Not a piastre. Allah—

EPIFANIA. Oh, bother Allah! What did you do with it?

THE DOCTOR. Allah is never bothered. On that afternoon when you left me to earn your own living I called upon the Merciful, the Compassionate, to reveal to me whether you were not one of the strokes of his infinite humor. Then I sat down and took up a newspaper. And behold! a paragraph headed Wills and Bequests. I read a name that I cannot remember: Mrs Somebody of Clapham Park, one hundred and twentytwo thousand pounds. She had never done anything but live in Clapham Park; and she left £122,000. But what was the next name? It was that of the teacher who changed my whole life and gave me a new soul by opening the world of science to me. I was his assistant for four years. He used to make his own apparatus for his experiments; and one day he needed a filament of metal that would resist a temperature that melted platinum like sealing wax.

EPIFANIA. Buy his patent for me if it has not been snapped up.

THE DOCTOR. He never took out a patent. He believed that knowledge is no man's property. And he had neither time nor money to waste in patent offices. Millions have been made out of that discovery of his by people who care nothing about science and everything about money. He left four hundred pounds and a widow: the good woman who had been a second mother to me. A shilling a day for her at most: not even one piastre an hour.

EPIFANIA. That comes of marrying an incompetent dreamer. Are you going to beg for her? I warn you I am tired of destitute widows. I should be a beggar myself if I took them all on my shoulders.

THE DOCTOR. Have no fear. The Merciful, the Compassionate heard the prayer of the widow. Listen. I once cured a Prime Minister when he imagined himself to be ill. I went to him and told him that it was the will of Allah that the widow should have a civil list pension. She received it: a hundred pounds a year. I went to the great Metallurgical Trust which exploits his discovery, and told them that her poverty was a scandal in the face of Allah. They were rich and generous: they made a special issue of founders' shares for her, worth three hundred a year to her. They called it letting her in on the ground floor. May her prayers win them favor from Him save in whom there is no might and no majesty! But all this took time. The illness, the nurse, the funeral, the disposal of the laboratory, the change to a cheaper lodging, had left her without a penny, though no doctor and no lawyer took a farthing, and the shopkeepers were patient; for the spirit of Allah worked more strongly upon them than on the British Treasury, which clamored for its little death duty. Between the death and the pensions there was a gap exactly one hundred and fifty pounds wide. He who is just and exact supplied that sum by your chauffeur's hands and by mine. It rejoiced my heart as money had never rejoiced it before. But instead of coming to you with fifty thousand pounds I am in arrear with my bill for my daily bread in your hotel, and am expecting every day to be told by your manager that this cannot go on: I must settle.

ALASTAIR. Well, old man, you may not have done a lot for yourself; but you have done damned well for the widow. And you have escaped Eppy. She wont marry you with your pockets empty.

EPIFANIA. Pray why? Fifty thousand pounds must have been made out of that discovery ten times over. The doctor, in putting my money into the widow's necessary expenses, may be said to have made a retrospective investment in the discovery. And he has shewn the greatest ability in the affair: has he not, Mr Sagamore?

SAGAMORE. Unquestionably. He has bowled out the Prime Minister. He has bowled out the Imperial Metallurgical Trust.

He has settled the widow's affairs to perfection.

THE DOCTOR. But not my own affairs. I am in debt for my food.

EPIFANIA. Well, if you come to that, *I* am in debt for my food. I got a letter this morning from my purveyors to say that I have paid them nothing for two years, and unless I let them have something on account they will be obliged to resort to the premises.

THE DOCTOR. What does that mean?

EPIFANIA. Sell my furniture.

THE DOCTOR. You cannot sell mine, I am afraid. I have hardly any.

BLENDERBLAND. If you have a stick she will sell it. She is the meanest woman in England.

EPIFANIA. That is why I am also the richest. Mr Sagamore: my mind is made up: I will marry this doctor. Ascertain his name and make the necessary arrangements.

BLENDERBLAND. You take care, doctor. She is unfaithful to her husband in wanting to marry you. She flirted with me: took me down the river and made me believe I was to be Alastair's successor before ever she saw you. See what she has done to me! She will do it to you when the next man takes her fancy.

THE DOCTOR [*to Epifania*] What have you to say to that?

EPIFANIA. You must learn to take chances in this world. This disappointed philanderer tries to frighten you with my unfaithfulness. He has never been married: I have. And I tell you that in the very happiest marriages not a day passes without a thousand moments of unfaithfulness. You begin by thinking you have only one husband: you find you have a dozen. There is a creature you hate and despise and are tied to for life; and before breakfast is over the fool says something nice and becomes a man whom you admire and love; and between these extremes there are a thousand degrees with a different man and woman at each of them. A wife is all women to one man: she is everything that is devilish: the thorn in his flesh, the jealous termagant, the detective dogging all his movements, the nagger, the scolder, the worrier. He has only to tell her an affectionate lie and she is his comfort, his helper,

THE MILLIONAIRESS

BLENDERBLAND. The Russians would shoot you as they would a mad dog. You are a bloated capitalist, you know.

EPIFANIA. I am a capitalist here; but in Russia I should be a worker. And what a worker! My brains are wasted here: the wealth they create is thrown away on idlers and their parasites, whilst poverty, dirt, disease, misery and slavery surround me like a black sea in which I may be engulfed at any moment by a turn of the money market. Russia needs managing women like me. In Moscow I shall not be a millionairess; but I shall be in the Sovnarkom within six months and in the Politbureau before the end of the year. Here I have no real power, no real freedom, and no security at all: we may all die in the workhouse. In Russia I shall have such authority! such scope for my natural powers! as the Empress Catharine never enjoyed. I swear that before I have been twenty years in Russia every Russian baby shall weigh five pounds heavier and every Russian man and woman live ten years longer. I shall not be an empress; and I may work myself to death; but in a thousand years from now holy Russia shall again have a patron saint, and her name shall be Saint Epifania.

BLENDERBLAND. The egotism of that woman!!

SAGAMORE. I am afraid there are no saints now in Russia.

THE DOCTOR. There are saints everywhere: they are the one species you cannot liquidate. Kings, emperors, conquerors, pontiffs and all the other idols are swept away sooner or later; and all the king's horses and all the king's men cannot set them up again; but the saints shall reign for ever and ever in the temple of the hammer and the sickle. But we must not go to Russia, because the Russians do not need us: they have stayed at home and saved their own souls. Ought not we to stay at home and save ours? Why not make the British Empire a Soviet republic?

EPIFANIA. By all means; but we shall have to liquidate all the adult inhabitants and begin with the newly born. And the first step to that is to get married. Mr Sagamore: make the necessary arrangements.

SAGAMORE [bows]!

PATRICIA. Congratulations, darling.